master
Scale & chord guide

2ND EDITION

for keyboard

ISBN 978-0-7935-6944-1

HAL•LEONARD®
CORPORATION

7777 W. BLUEMOUND RD. P.O. BOX 13819 MILWAUKEE, WI 53213

In Australia Contact:
Hal Leonard Australia Pty. Ltd.
4 Lentara Court
Cheltenham, Victoria, 3192 Australia
Email: ausadmin@halleonard.com

Visit Hal Leonard Online at
www.halleonard.com

PART ONE: SCALES AND KEYS
Major Scale Construction

The word **scale** comes from the Latin "scala," which means "ladder." A scale is a ladder of tones. The steps from one tone to the next fall into two categories: 1) the **half step,** which is the distance between two adjacent keys on the keyboard (with no keys in between); and 2) the **whole step,** which equals two half steps. Scales are constructed by a consistent pattern of half steps and whole steps, shown below.

C MAJOR SCALE

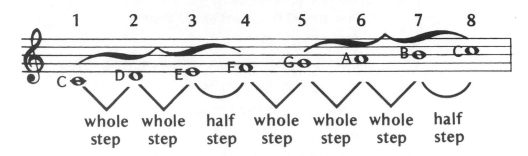

This pattern — whole, whole, half, whole, whole, whole, half — can be remembered more easily by dividing the scale into two groups of four notes. Each group has the pattern: whole, whole, half. A whole step separates the four-note groups.

The scale above is a **C** scale because it begins on C. C is called the "keynote," or "tonic." It is a **major** scale because of the interval from the tonic to the third note. An **interval** is simply the distance between two notes. Half steps and whole steps are intervals. The interval from the tonic to the third note of the scale is a **major third** (equal to two whole steps). Thus, the scale is called a major scale.

Each major scale has a **key signature** that reflects the sharps or flats in the scale that arise because of the pattern of whole and half steps. The C major scale has a key signature of no sharps or flats.

Minor Scales

In addition to major scales, there are **minor scales** — scales in which the third note is a **minor third** (one and one-half steps) above the tonic. For every major scale, there is a minor scale with the same key signature, called the **relative minor.** It begins two scale notes below the major scale.

A MINOR SCALE
(relative minor of C major)

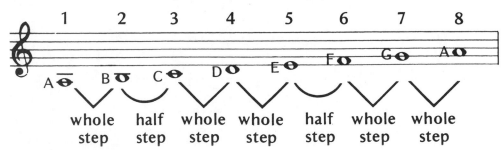

This form of the minor scale — called the **natural minor** — is often altered by raising the seventh note, and sometimes the sixth as well, one half step. These altered scale forms are known as the **harmonic minor** and the **melodic minor,** respectively.

The Circle Of Keys

The circle below illustrates the natural progression of keys at a glance.

- Moving clockwise — by ascending fifths — key signatures increase in the number of sharps (♯).

- Moving counterclockwise — by descending fifths — the key signatures increase in the number of flats (♭).

The keys on the lower part of the circle can be "spelled" either as sharp keys or as flat keys, depending on the direction from which they are approached. This difference in spelling is known as **enharmonic equivalence**, and it applies to individual notes as well as keys; for example, D♯ and E♭ are enharmonically equivalent, as are G♯ and A♭.

Outside the circle are the major keys (uppercase letters) with their relative minors (lowercase letters), and inside are the flats or sharps that form the key signatures.

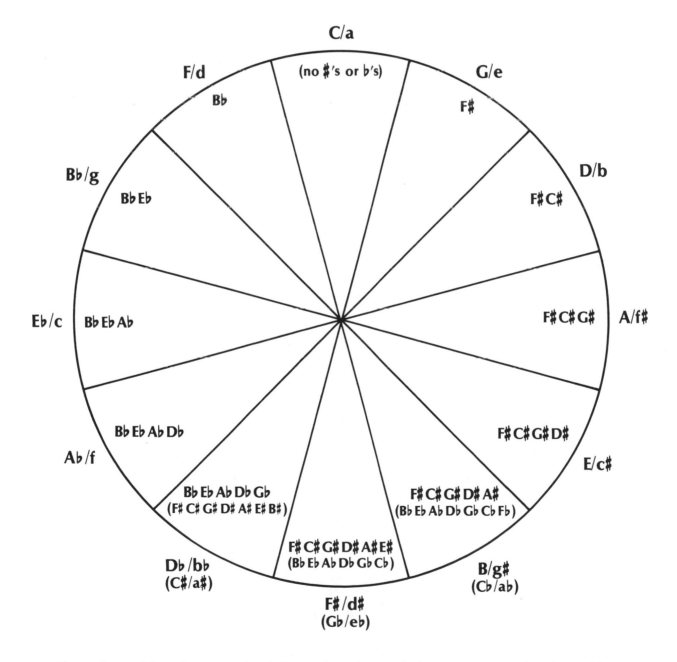

The scales and key signatures that follow reflect the clockwise sequence on the circle of keys.

Directory Of Scales And Key Signatures

Knowing what key you're playing in, and knowing the scale of that key, makes playing far easier than regarding the key signature as merely a collection of unrelated sharps or flats. To aid you in learning these scales — and to help you avoid fingering problems encountered in playing music — guideline fingering is given for each hand.

4

enharmonically
equivalent (see previous page)

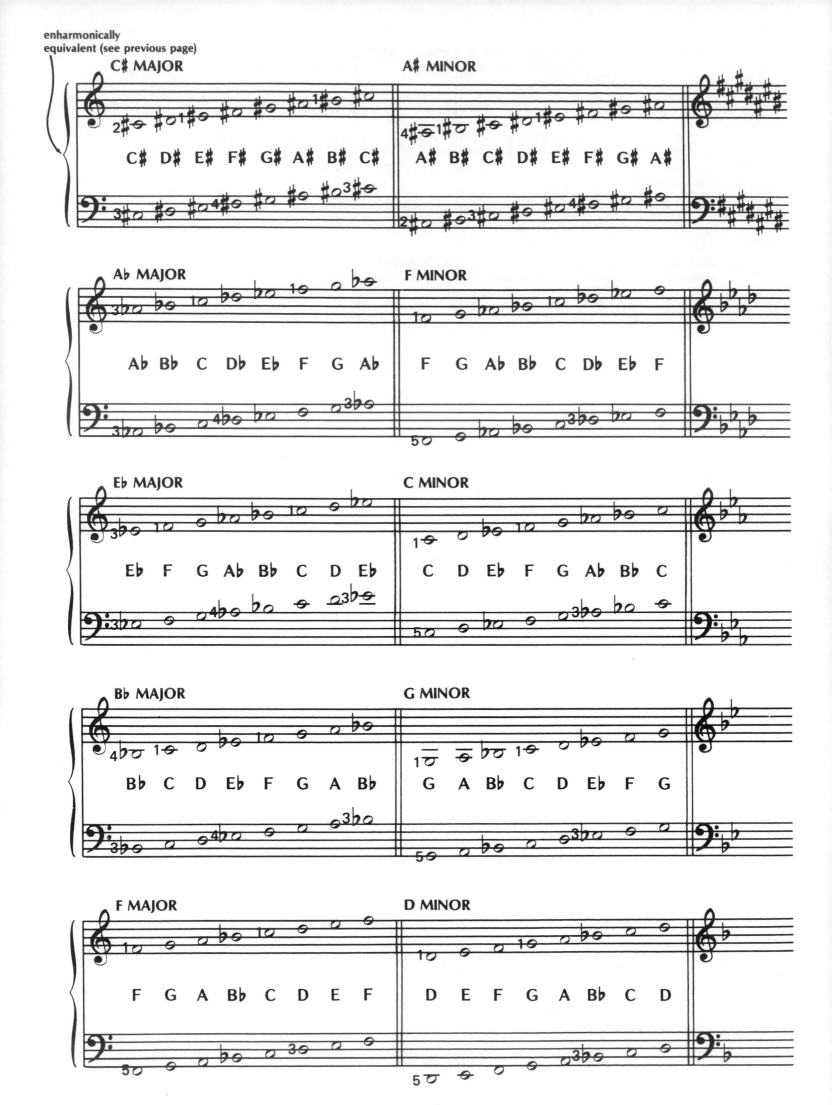

C♯ MAJOR

C♯ D♯ E♯ F♯ G♯ A♯ B♯ C♯

A♯ MINOR

A♯ B♯ C♯ D♯ E♯ F♯ G♯ A♯

Ab MAJOR

Ab Bb C Db Eb F G Ab

F MINOR

F G Ab Bb C Db Eb F

Eb MAJOR

Eb F G Ab Bb C D Eb

C MINOR

C D Eb F G Ab Bb C

Bb MAJOR

Bb C D Eb F G A Bb

G MINOR

G A Bb C D Eb F G

F MAJOR

F G A Bb C D E F

D MINOR

D E F G A Bb C D

PART TWO: CHORDS
Basic Chord Construction — Major And Minor Triads

In written music, accompaniment harmony is often indicated by abbreviated **chord symbols** appearing above the staff. This part of the book concerns translating these symbols into notes on the keyboard.

Chords are constructed using intervals of a third, of which there are two kinds: major (equal to two whole steps) and minor (equal to one and one-half steps). The most basic chords are **triads,** which means they consist of three notes.

The note upon which the chord is built is called the **root;** this note gives the chord its letter name. A third above the root is, naturally enough, the **third** of the chord. If the interval from the root to the third is major, it is a major chord; if it is minor, the chord is minor. Another third higher is the **fifth** of the chord, so called because of the interval it forms with the root.

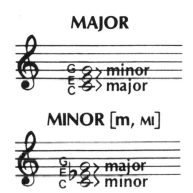

Notice that each kind of triad consists of a major and a minor third, and that the lower of these determines the type of chord. Throughout this book, chord symbols are given in parentheses for each chord type. Root names without additional qualification indicate major triads.

Of course, the way chords are constructed is not always the way they are used in music. By raising or lowering one or more chord tones by an octave, different chord positions, or **inversions,** are created. While the term "inversion" strictly refers to the use of a chord tone other than the root in the bass, it is applied in a looser sense to keyboard positions regardless of the bass note.

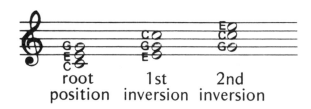

root position   1st inversion   2nd inversion

The chord charts which form the greater part of this book show common chords in all inversions, in both treble and bass clef.

The root and fifth are the most common bass notes for major and minor triads, as well as for the higher chord forms which are based on them.

Higher Chord Forms — Major

MAJOR SEVENTH
[maj 7, MA7]

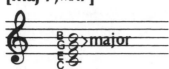

This chord adds a major third above the major triad. The new note is the **major seventh** of the chord, since it lies at the interval of a major seventh above the root.

MAJOR NINTH
[maj 9, MA9]

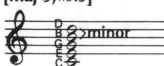

A minor third added above the major seventh chord. Pianists generally play the root with the left hand, and the remainder of the chord with the right.

SEVENTH [7]

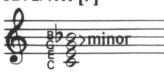

A minor third added above the major triad. Sometimes called a **dominant seventh** chord, since its root is often the fifth note (dominant) of the scale, it tends to lead into the chord on the first note (tonic) of the scale; e.g., C7→F. The remaining major-form chords are dominant chords also.

NINTH [9]

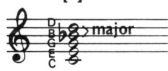

A major third added above the seventh chord. Notice that all notes added above triads alternate major and minor thirds. Distribute the parts as with the major ninth chord.

ELEVENTH [11]

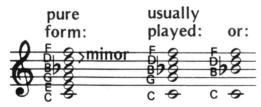

The pure form of this chord adds a minor third above the ninth chord (again, note the alternation of major and minor thirds), but is usually simplified by removing the third of the chord, and sometimes the fifth as well. Distribute the parts as with the major ninth chord. See the sections on Additions And Alterations and Bass Notes Other Than The Root for more about this increasingly popular chord.

THIRTEENTH [13]

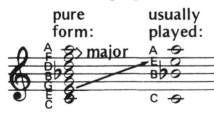

A major third above the eleventh chord forms the thirteenth, which is usually reduced as shown, with the third raised an octave. Distribute the parts as with major ninth chords. An alternative is to play a simple seventh chord, since the thirteenth is almost invariably in the melody when this symbol appears.

Higher Chord Forms — Minor

MINOR WITH MAJOR (SHARPED) SEVENTH
[m#7, m(+7), MI(MA7)]

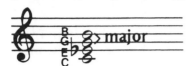

Add a major third above the minor triad.

MINOR SEVENTH
[m7, MI7]

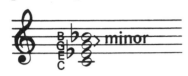

Add a minor third above the minor triad.

MINOR NINTH
[m9, MI9]

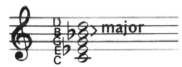

A major third added above the minor seventh chord.

Additions And Alterations

SIXTH [6]

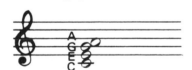

Add the note a whole step above the fifth of the major triad.

MINOR SIXTH
[m6, MI6]

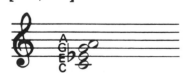

Add a whole step above the fifth of the minor triad.

SIXTH WITH ADDED NINTH [6/9]

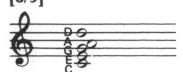

A major triad with a sixth and a ninth added.

SEVENTH WITH FLATTED FIFTH [7-5, 7(♭5)]

A seventh chord with the fifth lowered one-half step. The flatted fifth can also be considered the root; that is, the notes of C7-5 are enharmonically equivalent to those of G♭7-5.

MINOR SEVENTH WITH FLATTED FIFTH [m7-5 MI7(♭5)]

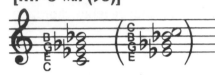

A minor seventh chord with the fifth lowered one-half step. Also called a **half-diminished chord** (see the section on Augmented And Diminished Chords). The third of the chord can be used in the bass, changing it into a minor sixth chord: Cm7-5 = E♭m6.

SEVENTH WITH FLATTED NINTH [7-9, 7(♭9)]

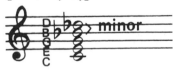

Lower the ninth of the ninth chord one-half step; i.e., add a minor third above a seventh chord.

SEVENTH WITH SHARP NINTH [7(♯9)]

correct   alternate
spelling: spelling:

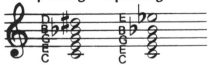

Raise the ninth of the ninth chord one-half step. The alternate spelling arises out of the use of the sharp ninth as a "blue note," which is a minor third played against a major chord. The fifth of the chord is often omitted.

SUSPENDED FOURTH [sus, sus4]

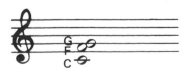

Raise the third of a major triad one-half step. The fourth is considered a **suspension** which usually resolves to a third. Seventh chords with a suspended fourth (7sus) are common. Ninth chords with a suspended fourth (9sus) are, for all practical purposes, the same as eleventh chords.

Augmented And Diminished Chords

AUGMENTED
[aug, +]

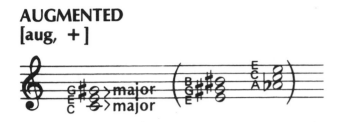

Raise the fifth of the major triad one-half step. Thus, the chord consists of two major thirds. Any of the three chord tones can be considered the root: C+ = E+ = A+. Augmented seventh chords (7+5, +7) are not uncommon.

DIMINISHED (SEVENTH)
[dim, dim 7, °]

This chord consists of three minor thirds. As with the augmented chord, any chord tone is a possible root. Rarely, this symbol calls for the bottom three notes only — a **diminished triad.** A diminished triad with a minor seventh is also common, being called a **half-diminished chord** (∅) or, usually, a **minor seventh chord with flatted fifth** (see Additions And Alterations).

Bass Notes Other Than The Root

The indication of bass notes other than the root, either parenthetically — C (E bass) — or via a "slash" — C/E — generally serves one of two purposes:

- to indicate an important bass line using a certain inversion of a chord, as illustrated above; or

- to notate complex chords more simply; e.g., Gm7/C = C11.

In connection with the second point, a couple of shortcuts will make some complex chords easier to remember:

- For eleventh chords, play the root in the bass and a minor seventh chord on the fifth (Gm7/C), **or** the root in the bass and a major triad on the note a whole step lower (Bb/C).

- For seventh chords with flatted ninth, play the root in the bass and a **diminished** chord on the fifth (G dim/C), **or,** keeping the root in the bass, play a seventh chord with the root raised one-half step.

PART THREE: CHORD CHARTS
C CHORDS

C MAJOR (C)	C MINOR (Cm, CMI)	C AUGMENTED (Caug, C+)
Root Position	**Root Position**	**Root Position**
1st Inversion	**1st Inversion**	**1st Inversion**
2nd Inversion	**2nd Inversion**	**2nd Inversion**

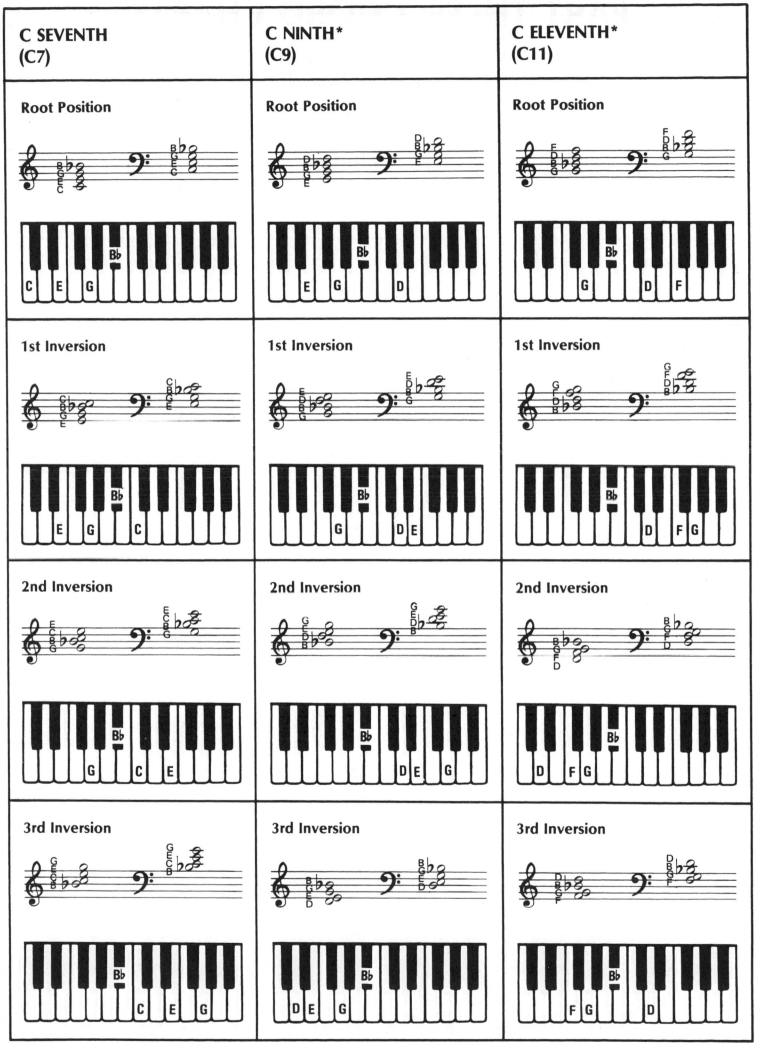

The ninth and eleventh chords do not include the root, which is assumed to be played in the bass.

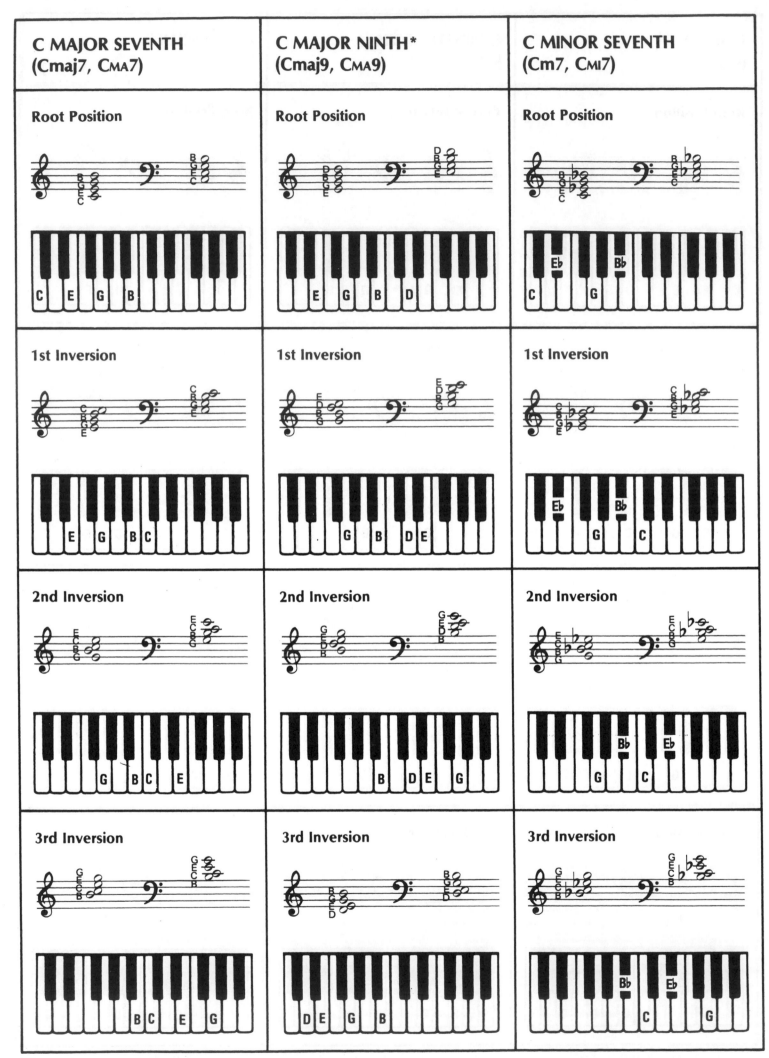

*See note on previous page.

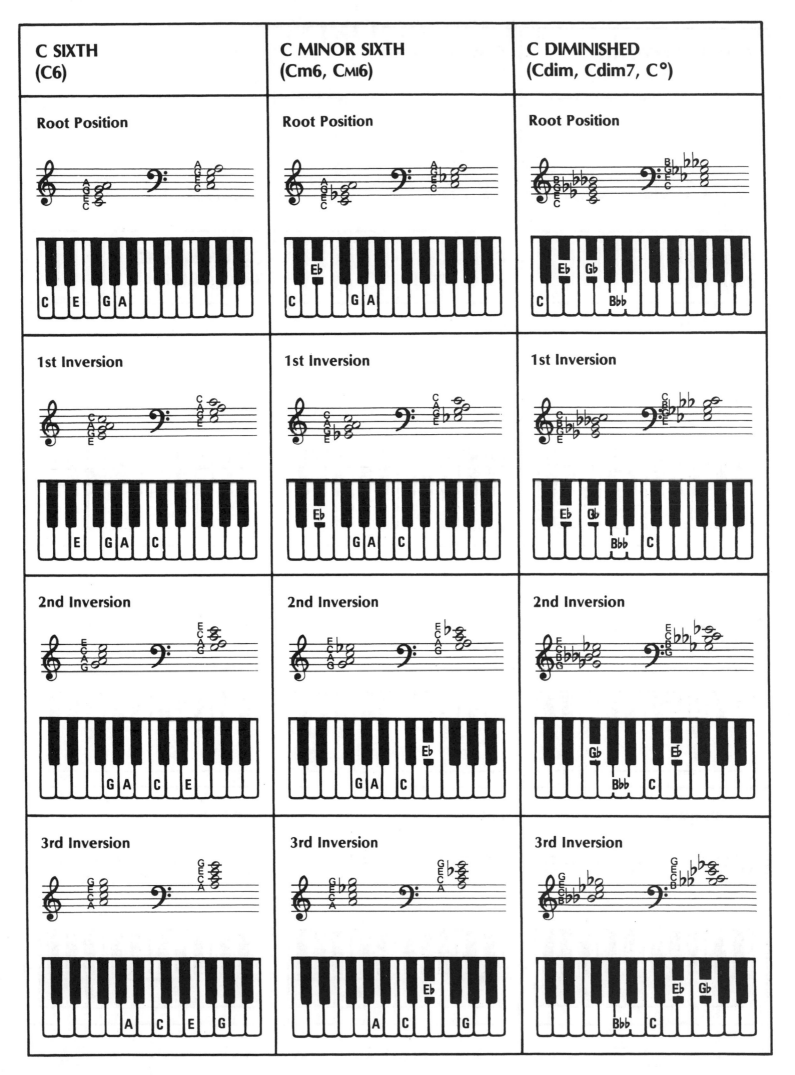

C#/Db CHORDS*

*C# and Db are enharmonically equivalent. For convenience' sake, all chords have been notated as C# chords.

C# MAJOR (C#)	C# MINOR (C#m, C#MI)	C# AUGMENTED (C#aug, C#+)
Root Position	**Root Position**	**Root Position**
1st Inversion	**1st Inversion**	**1st Inversion**
2nd Inversion	**2nd Inversion**	**2nd Inversion**

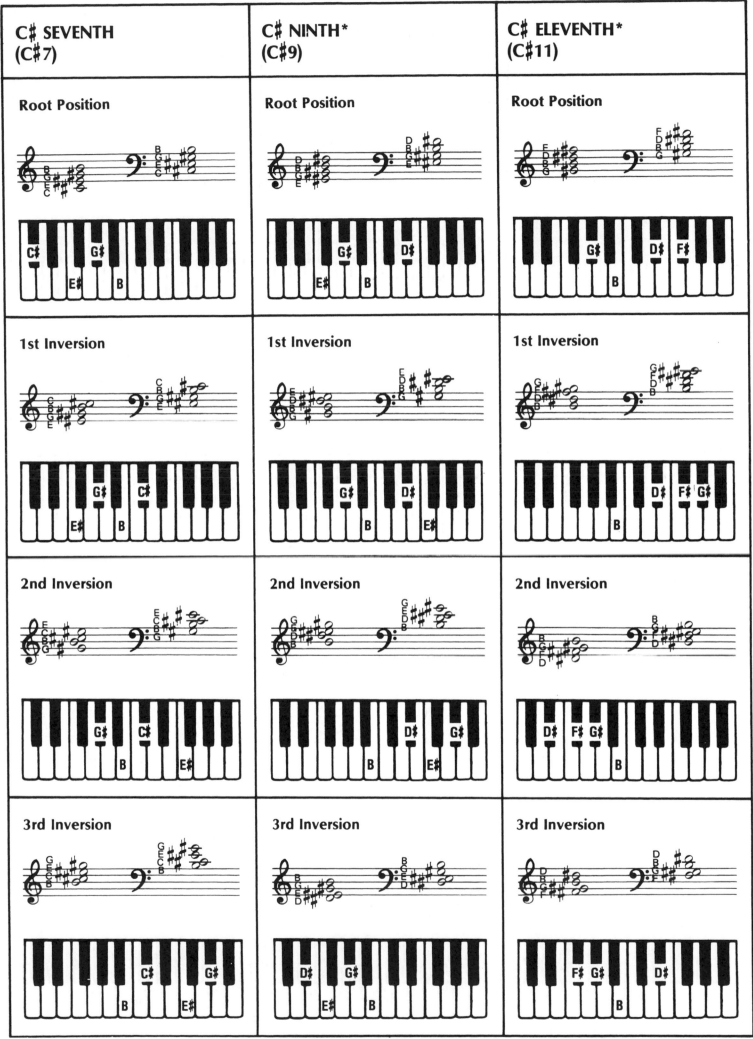

The ninth and eleventh chords do not include the root, which is assumed to be played in the bass.

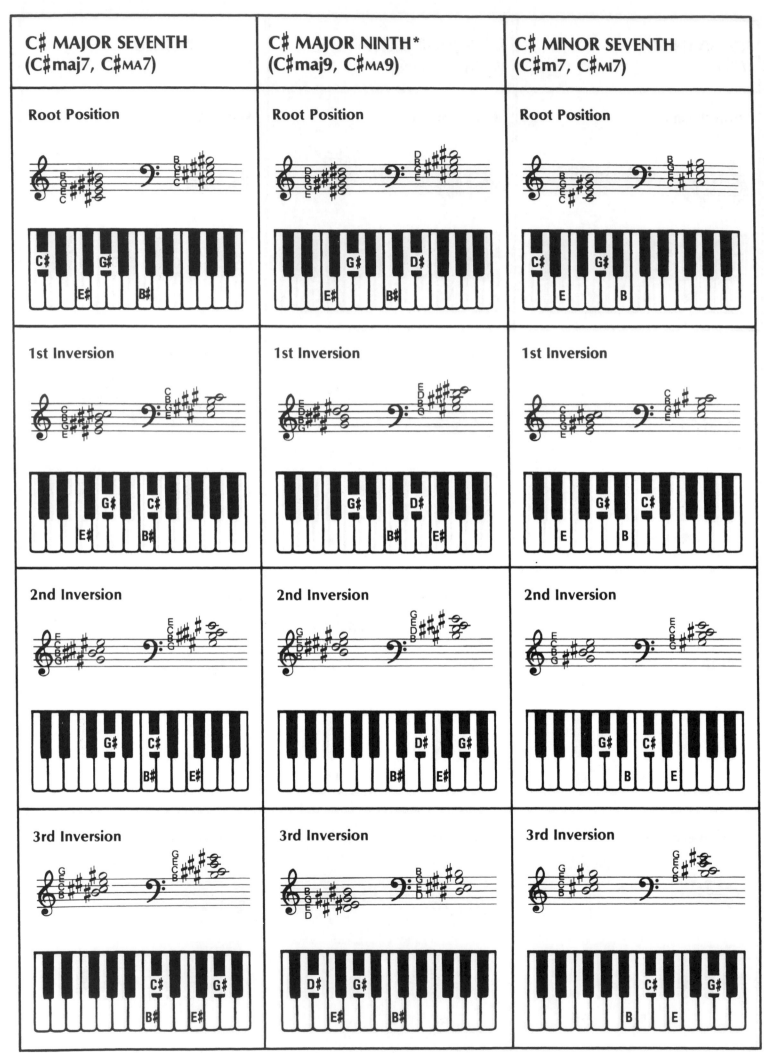

*See note on previous page.

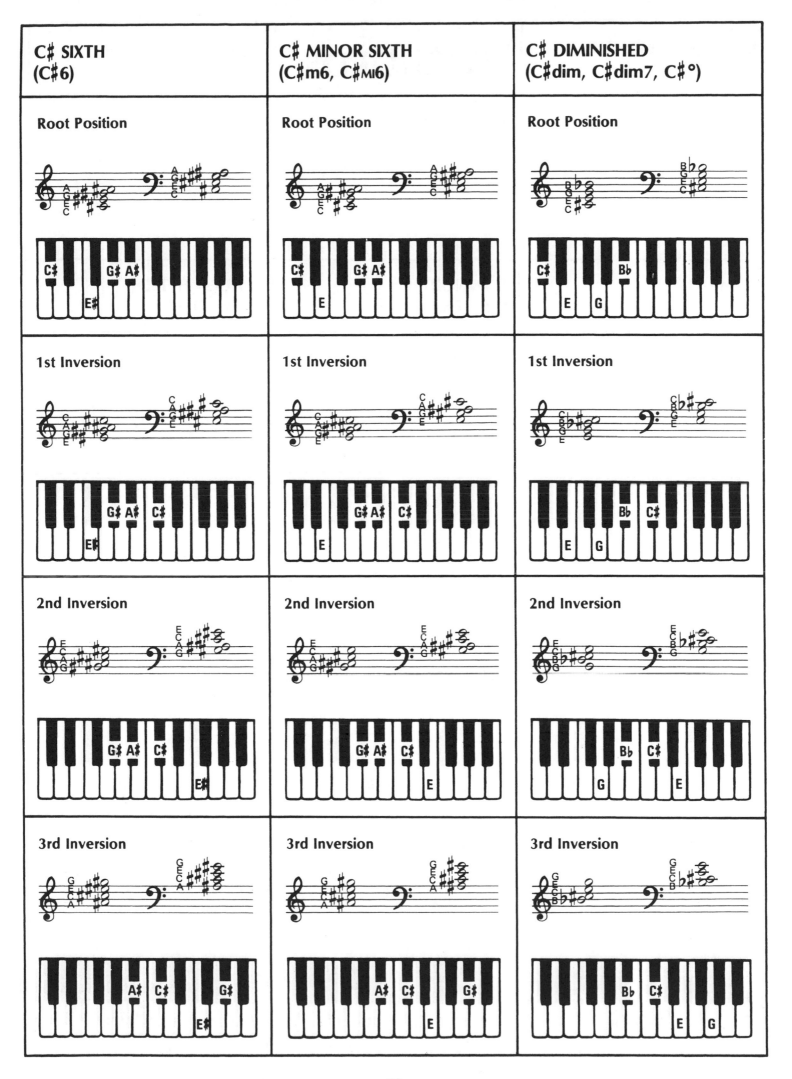

D CHORDS

D MAJOR (D)	D MINOR (Dm, Dᴍɪ)	D AUGMENTED (Daug, D +)
Root Position	**Root Position**	**Root Position**
1st Inversion	**1st Inversion**	**1st Inversion**
2nd Inversion	**2nd Inversion**	**2nd Inversion**

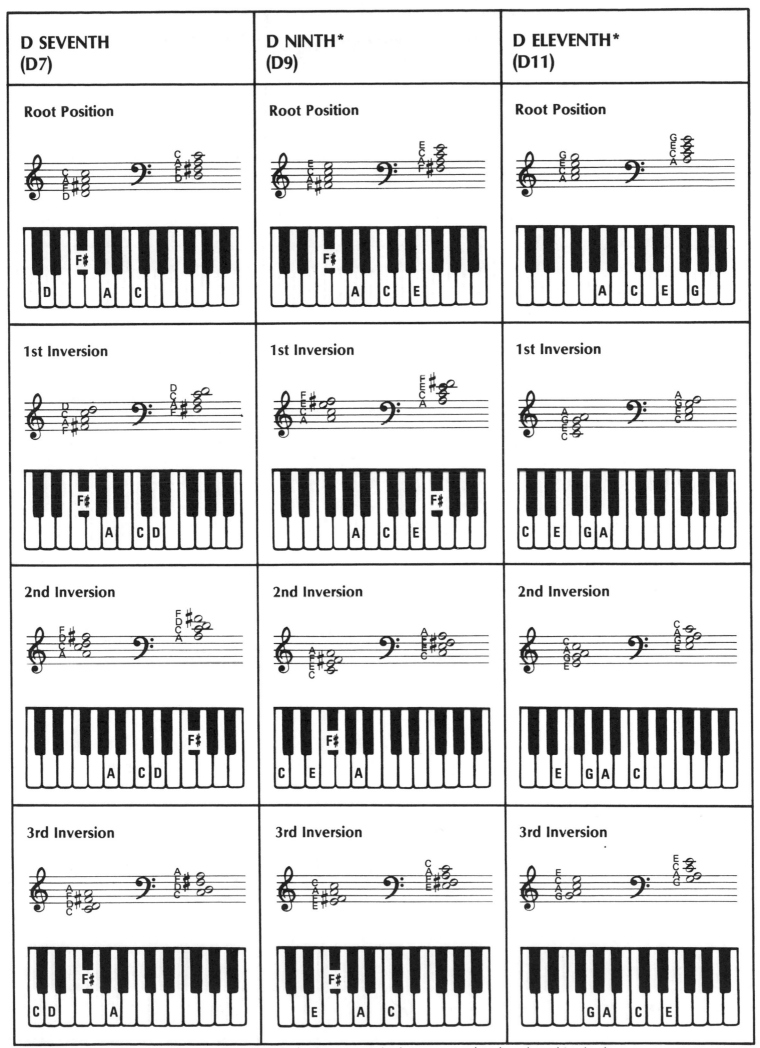

*The ninth and eleventh chords do not include the root, which is assumed to be played in the bass.

D MAJOR SEVENTH (Dmaj7, DMA7)	D MAJOR NINTH* (Dmaj9, DMA9)	D MINOR SEVENTH (Dm7, DMI7)

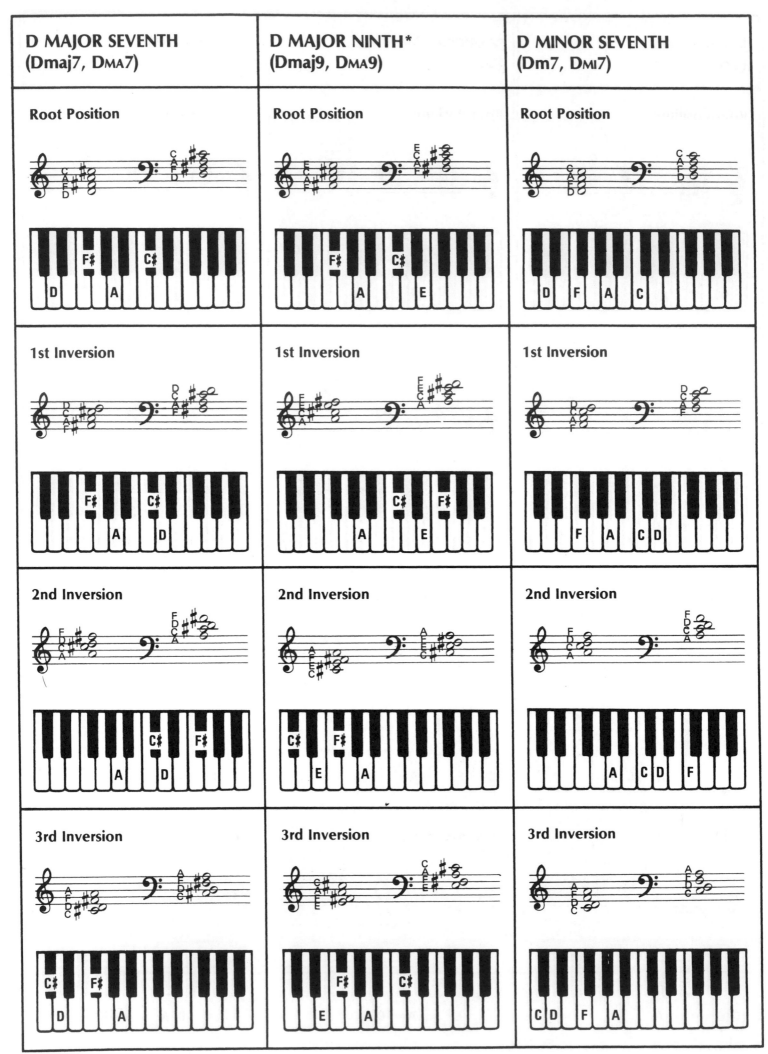

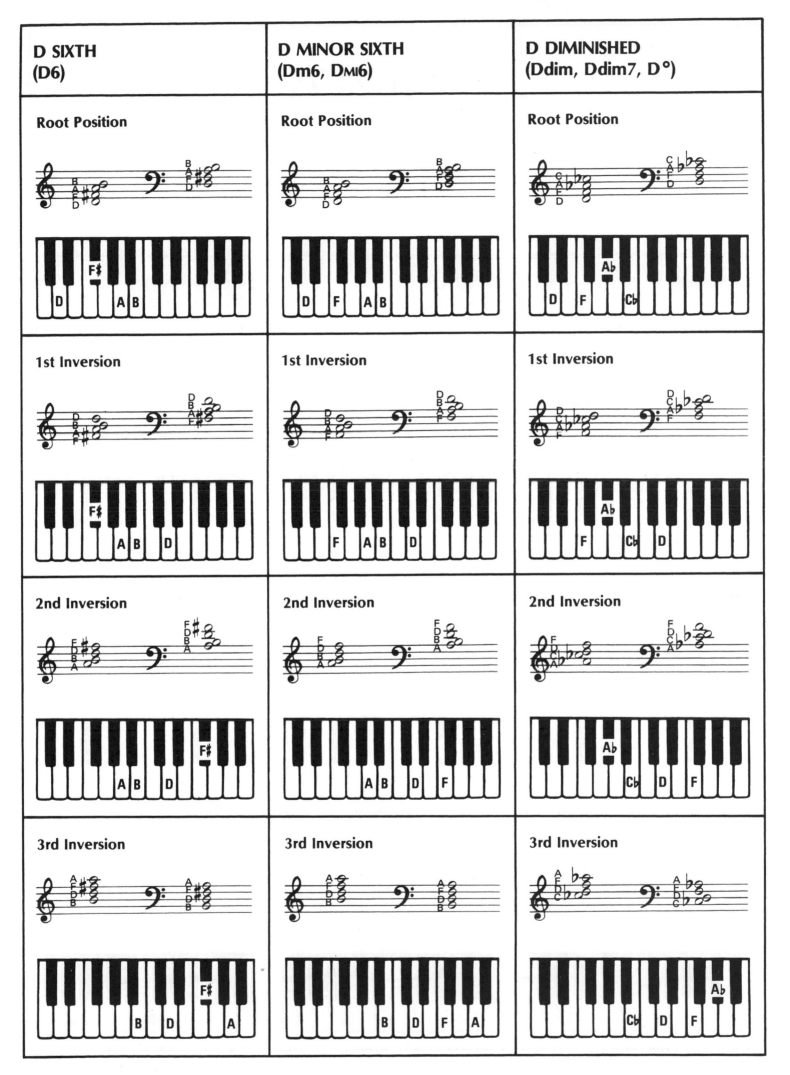

E♭ CHORDS

E♭ MAJOR (E♭)	E♭ MINOR (E♭m, E♭mi)	E♭ AUGMENTED (E♭aug, E♭ +)

Root Position

1st Inversion

2nd Inversion

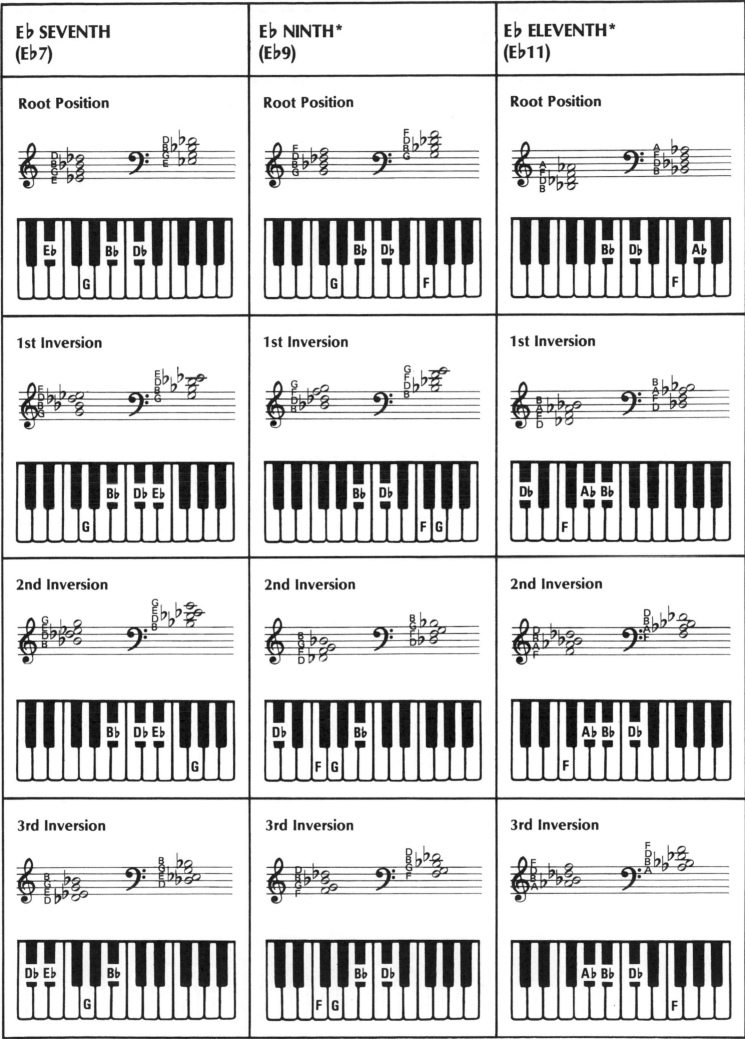

The ninth and eleventh chords do not include the root, which is assumed to be played in the bass.

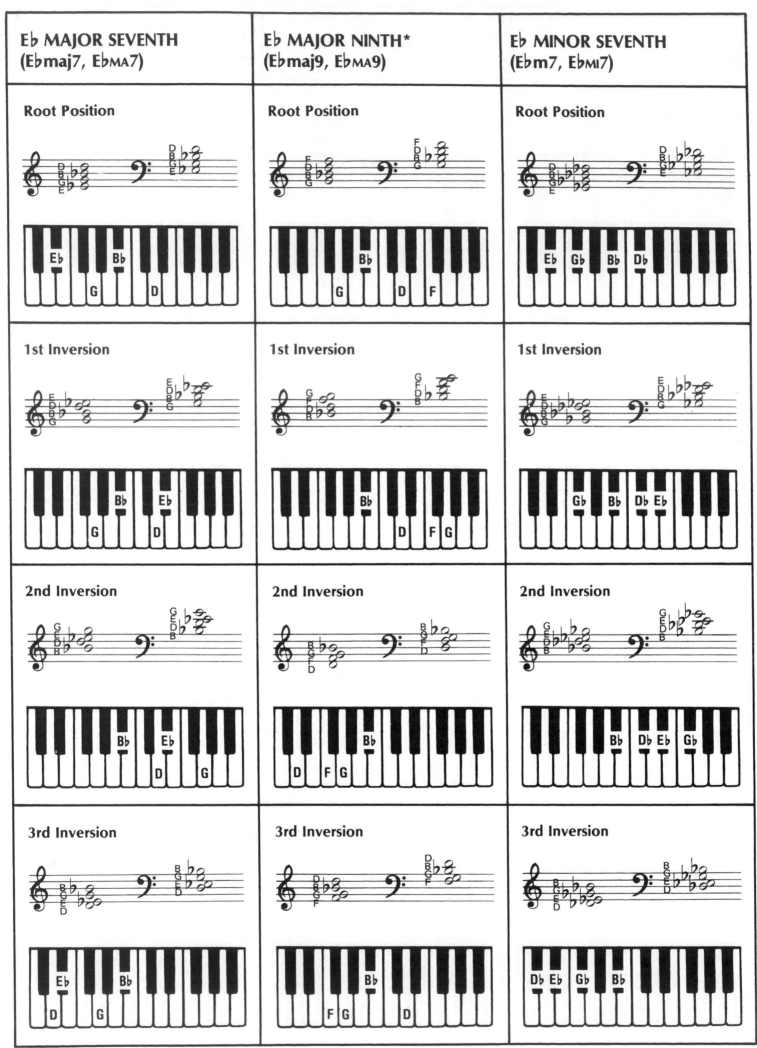

*See note on previous page.

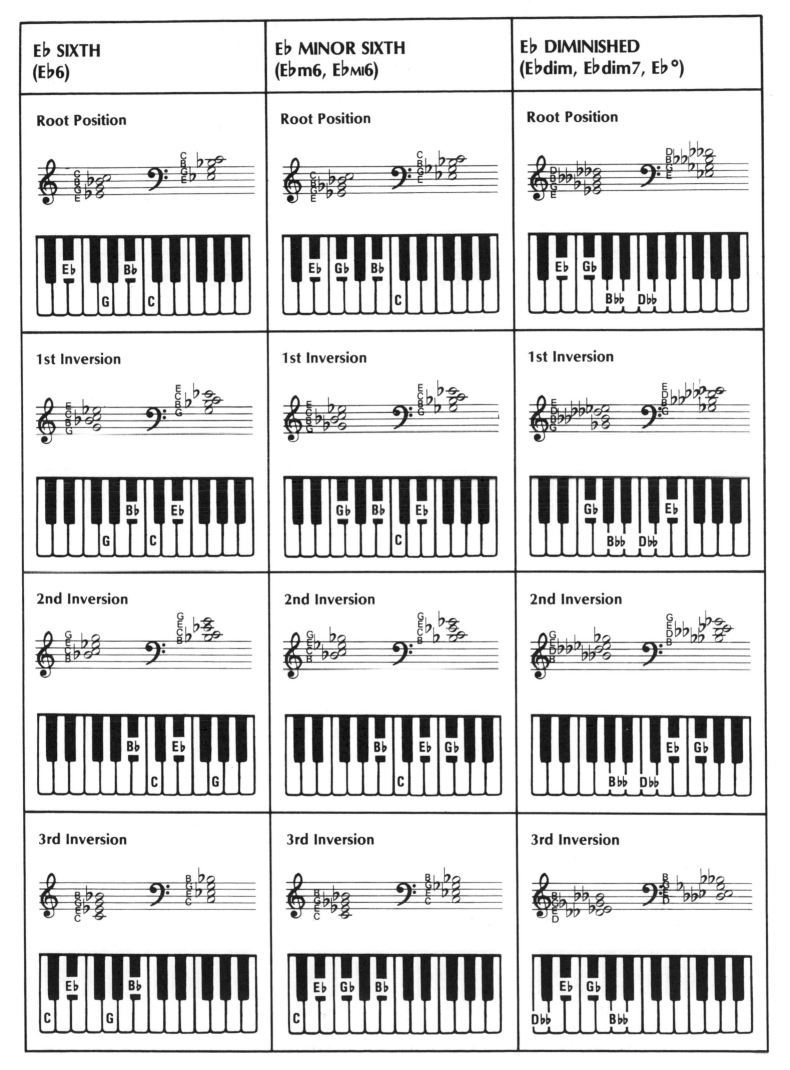

E CHORDS

E MAJOR (E)	E MINOR (Em, Emi)	E AUGMENTED (Eaug, E+)
Root Position	**Root Position**	**Root Position**
1st Inversion	**1st Inversion**	**1st Inversion**
2nd Inversion	**2nd Inversion**	**2nd Inversion**

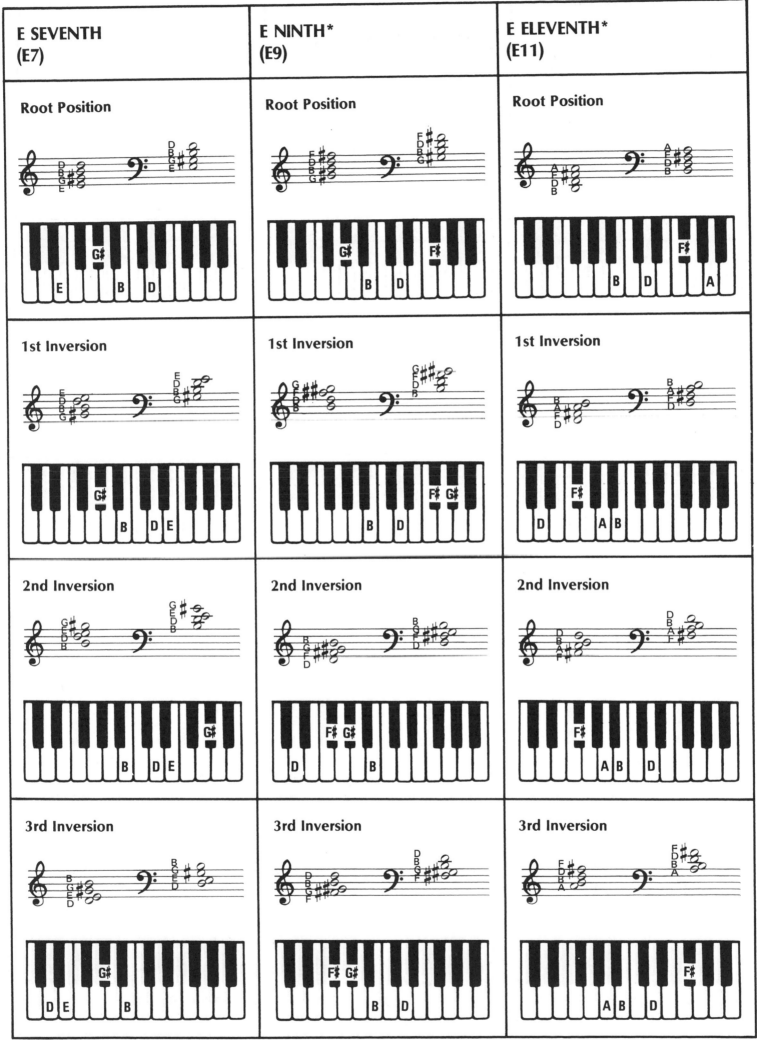

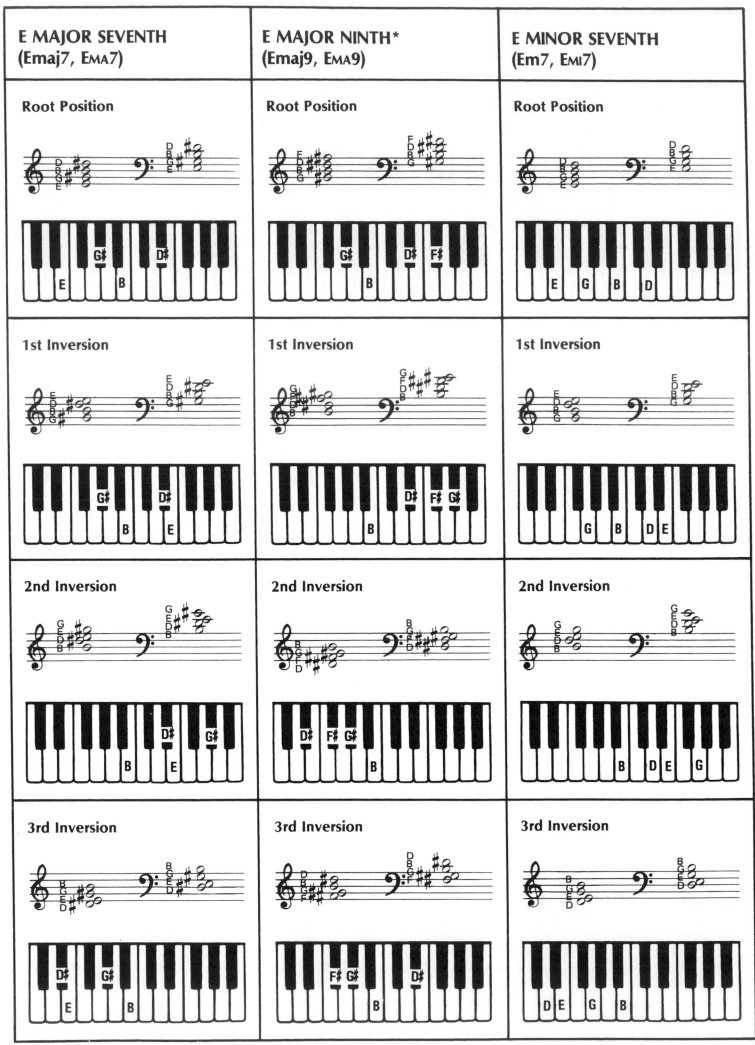

See note on previous page.

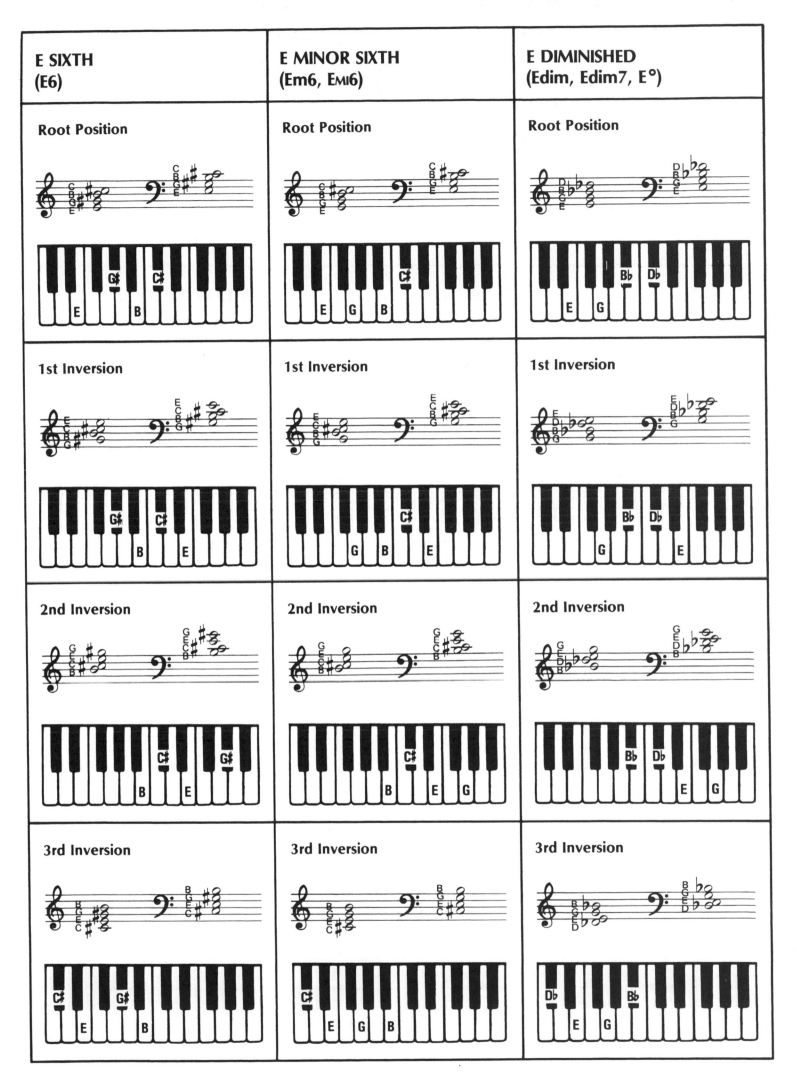

F CHORDS

F MAJOR (F)	F MINOR (Fm, FMI)	F AUGMENTED (Faug, F+)
Root Position	**Root Position**	**Root Position**
1st Inversion	**1st Inversion**	**1st Inversion**
2nd Inversion	**2nd Inversion**	**2nd Inversion**

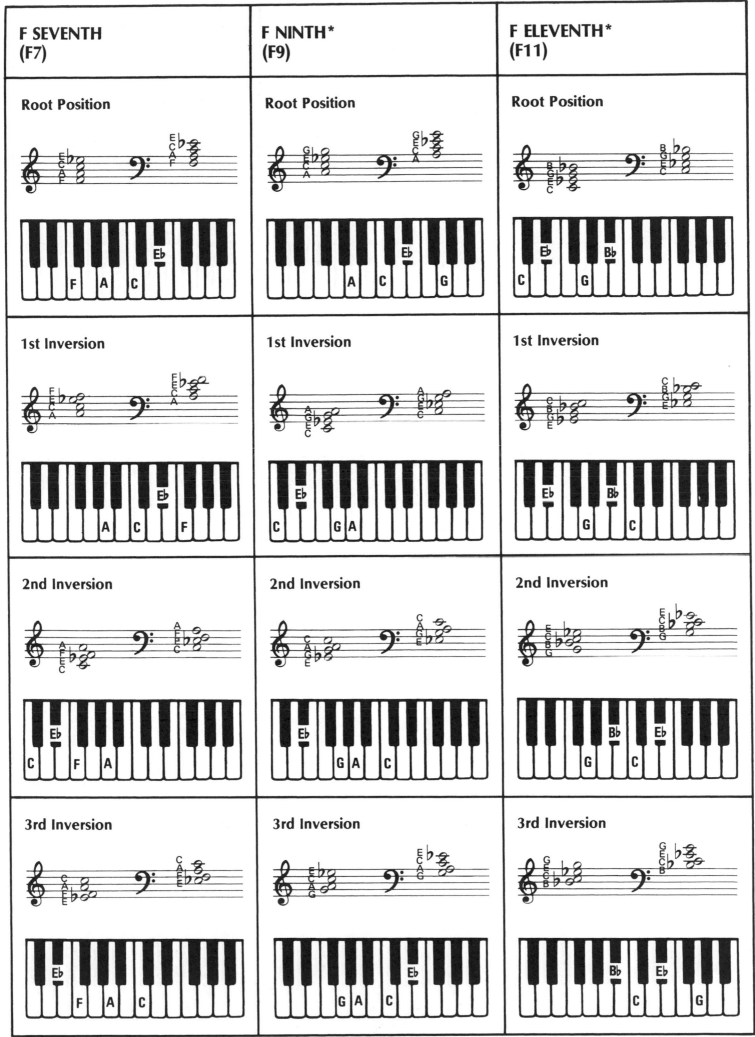

The ninth and eleventh chords do not include the root, which is assumed to be played in the bass.

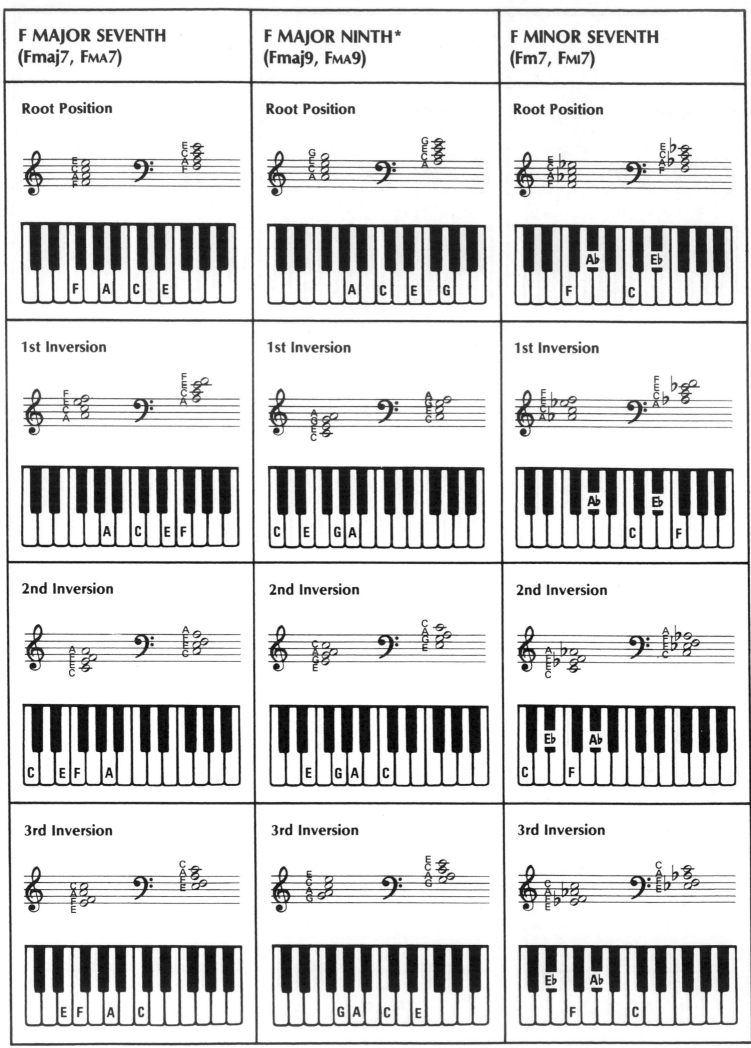

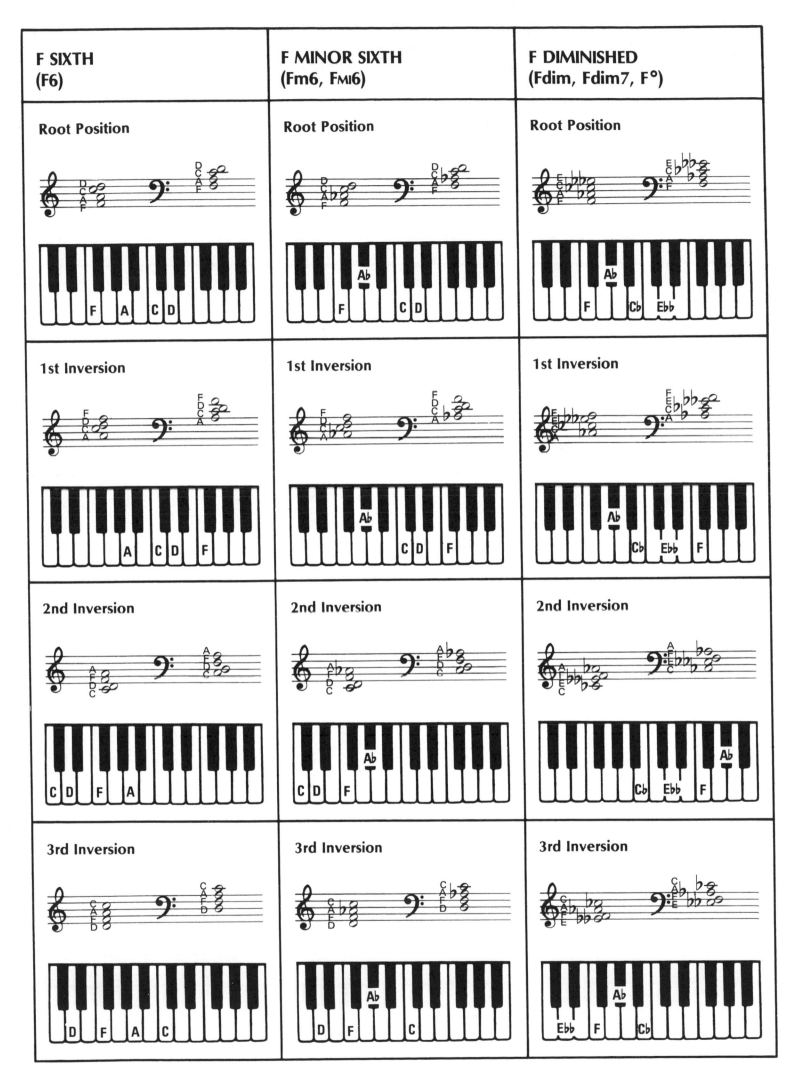

F#/Gb CHORDS*

F# and Gb are enharmonically equivalent. For convenience' sake, all chords have been notated as F# chords.

F# MAJOR (F#)	F# MINOR (F#m, F#MI)	F# AUGMENTED (F#aug, F# +)
Root Position	Root Position	Root Position
1st Inversion	1st Inversion	1st Inversion
2nd Inversion	2nd Inversion	2nd Inversion

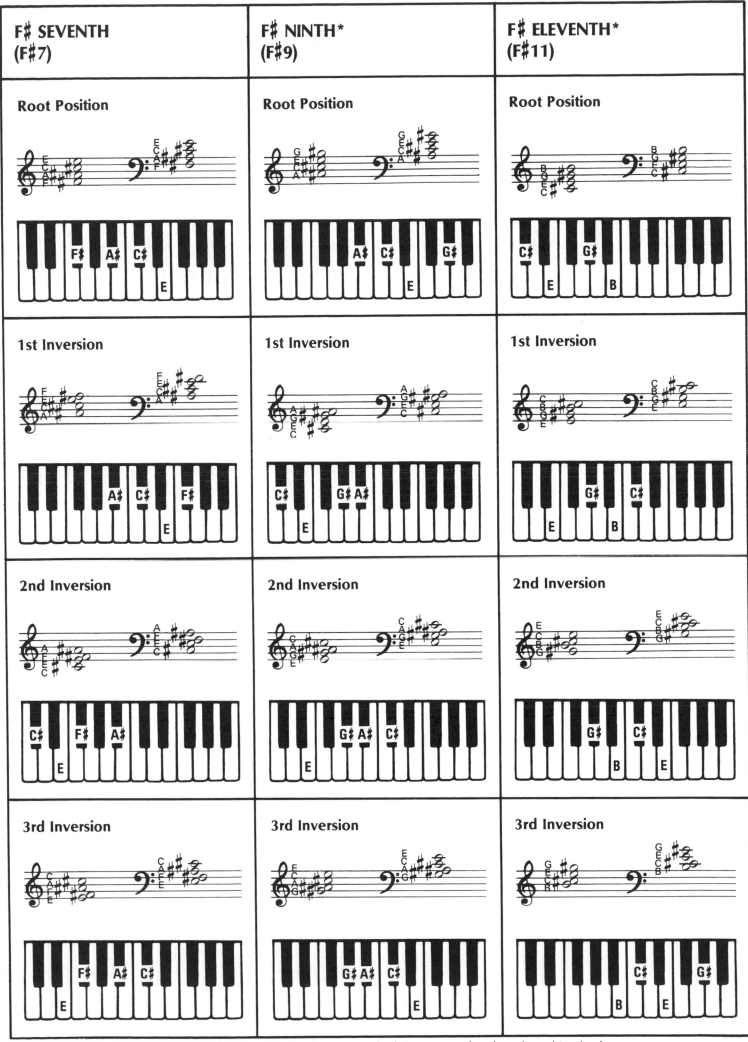

F# SEVENTH (F#7)	F# NINTH* (F#9)	F# ELEVENTH* (F#11)
Root Position	Root Position	Root Position
1st Inversion	1st Inversion	1st Inversion
2nd Inversion	2nd Inversion	2nd Inversion
3rd Inversion	3rd Inversion	3rd Inversion

The ninth and eleventh chords do not include the root, which is assumed to be played in the bass.

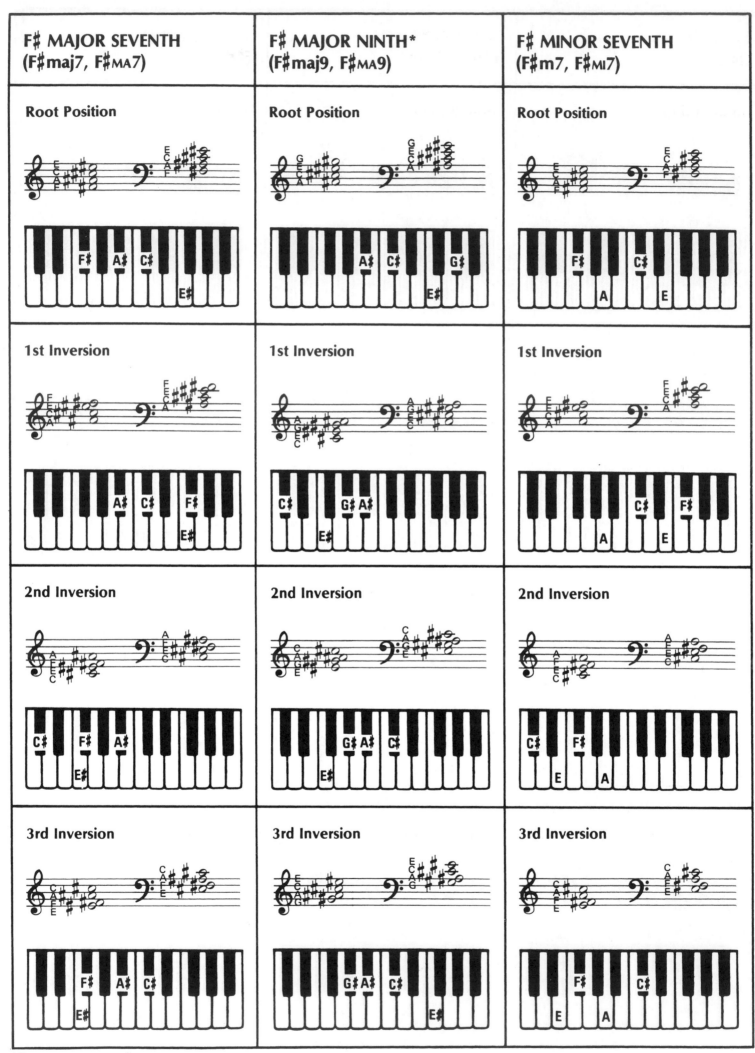

See note on previous page.

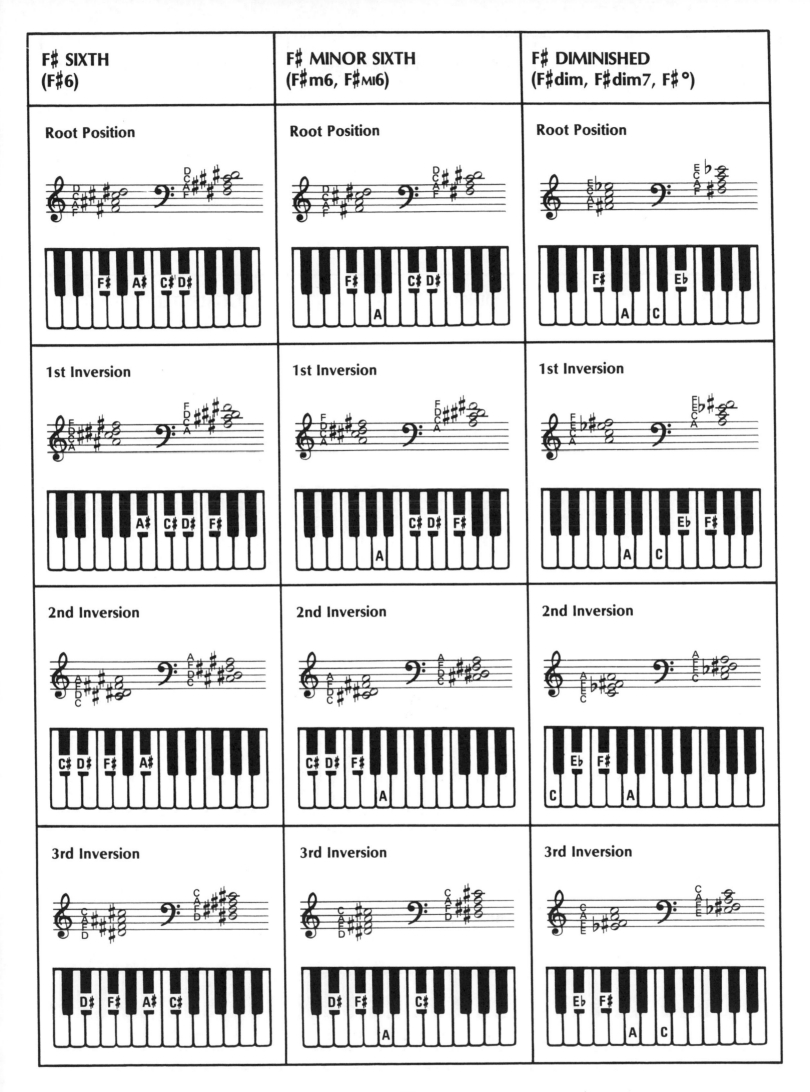

G CHORDS

G MAJOR (G)	G MINOR (Gm, GMI)	G AUGMENTED (Gaug, G+)
Root Position	**Root Position**	**Root Position**
1st Inversion	**1st Inversion**	**1st Inversion**
2nd Inversion	**2nd Inversion**	**2nd Inversion**

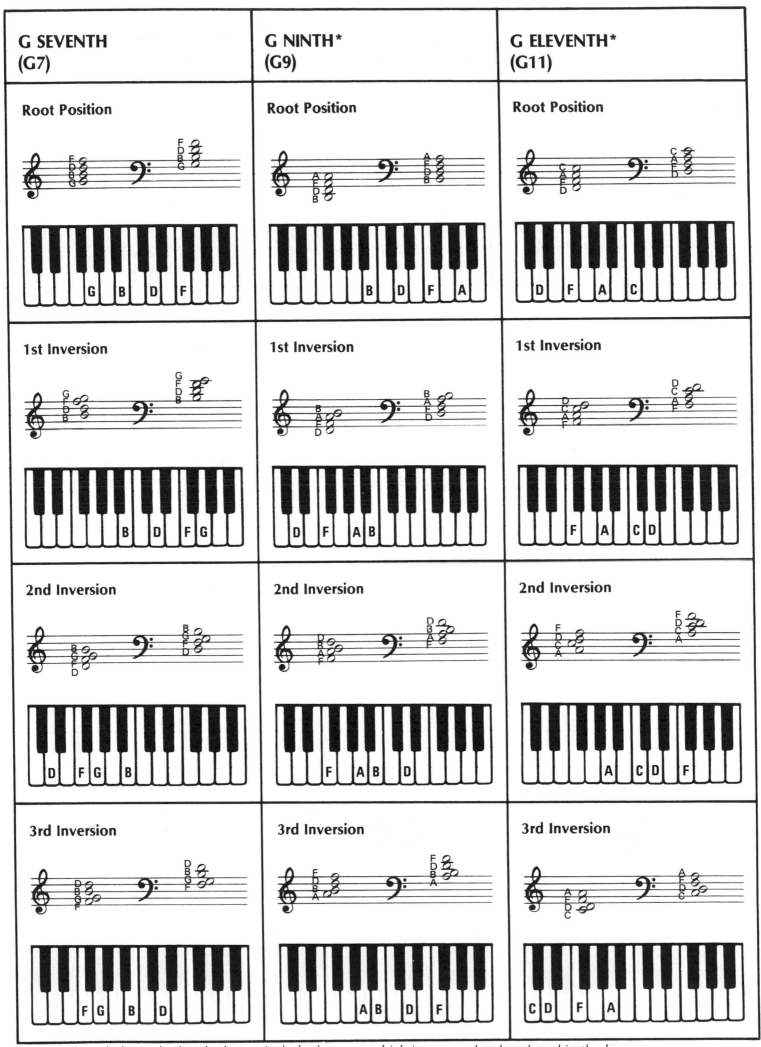

The ninth and eleventh chords do not include the root, which is assumed to be played in the bass.

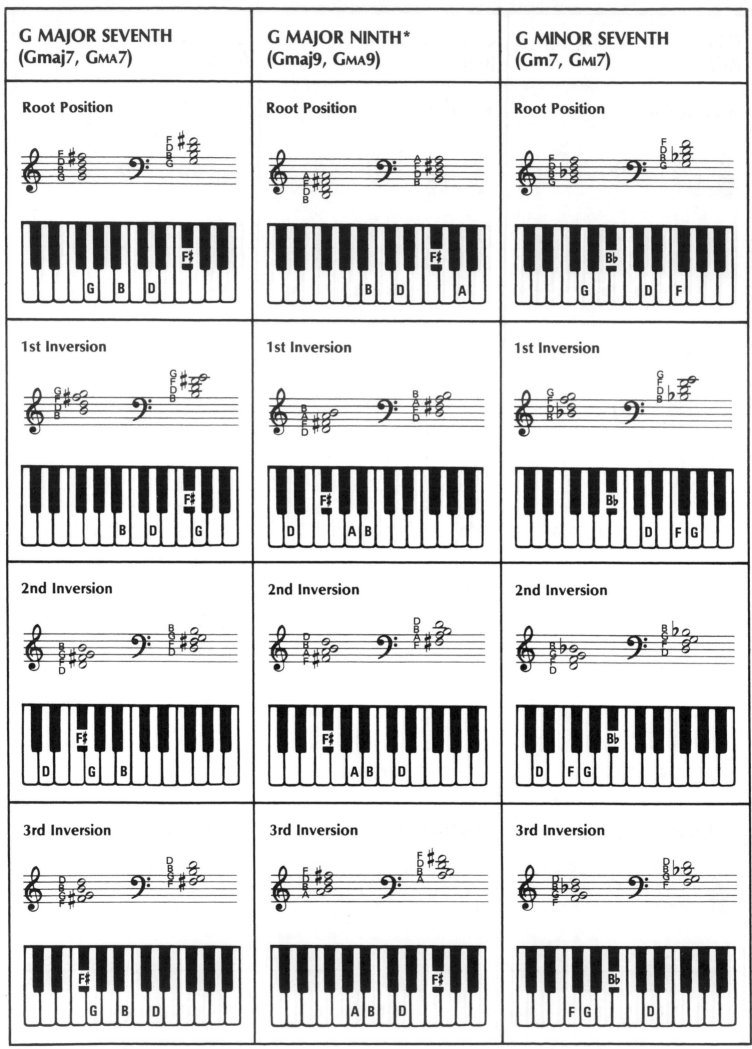

G MAJOR SEVENTH (Gmaj7, GMA7)	G MAJOR NINTH* (Gmaj9, GMA9)	G MINOR SEVENTH (Gm7, GMI7)
Root Position	Root Position	Root Position
1st Inversion	1st Inversion	1st Inversion
2nd Inversion	2nd Inversion	2nd Inversion
3rd Inversion	3rd Inversion	3rd Inversion

*See note on previous page.

42

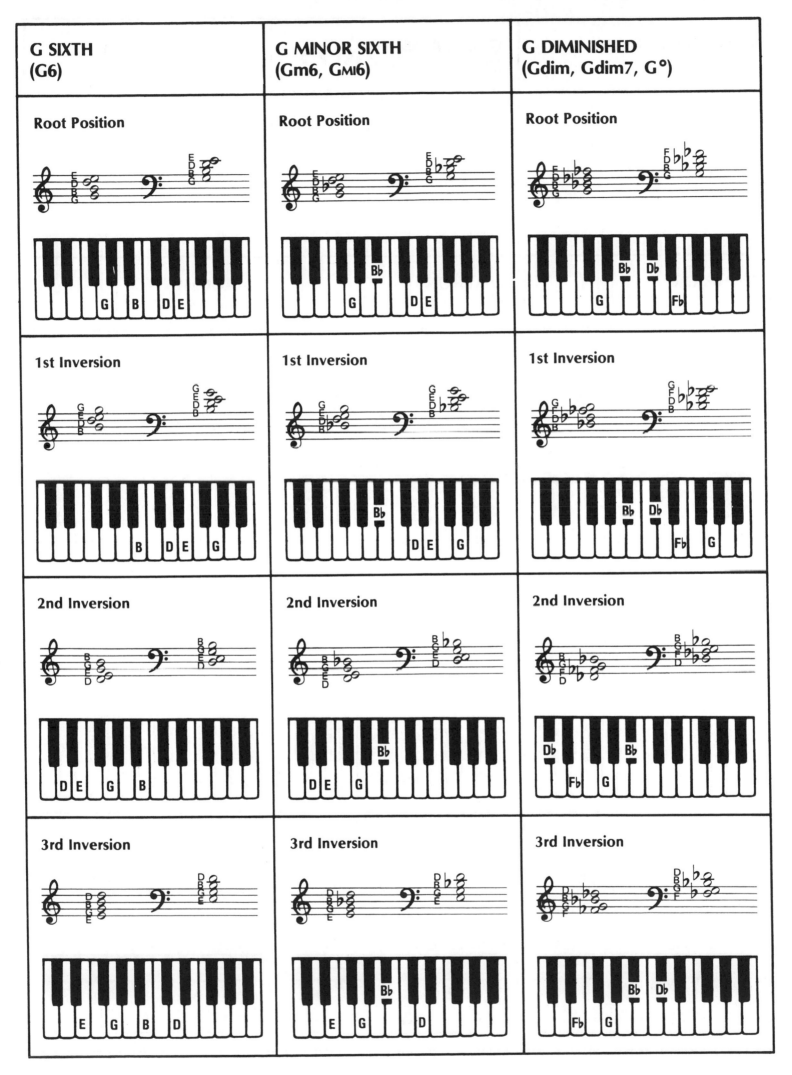

A♭ CHORDS

A♭ MAJOR (A♭)	A♭ MINOR (A♭m, A♭mi)	A♭ AUGMENTED (A♭aug, A♭+)
Root Position	**Root Position**	**Root Position**
1st Inversion	**1st Inversion**	**1st Inversion**
2nd Inversion	**2nd Inversion**	**2nd Inversion**

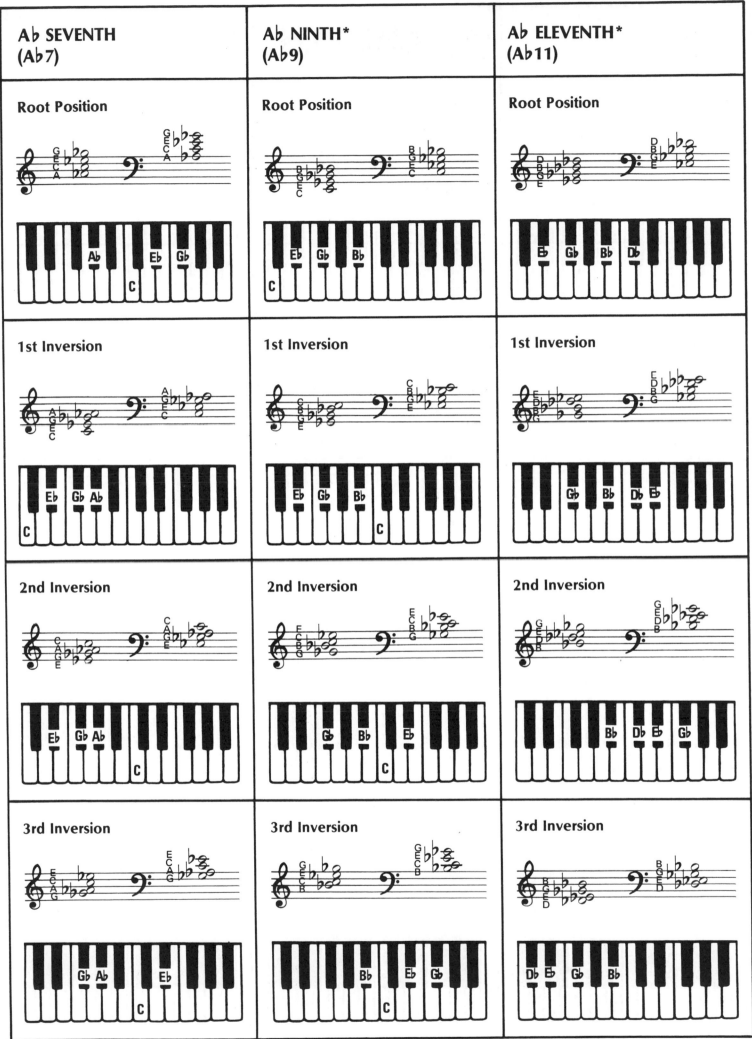

Ab SEVENTH (Ab7)	Ab NINTH* (Ab9)	Ab ELEVENTH* (Ab11)
Root Position	**Root Position**	**Root Position**
1st Inversion	**1st Inversion**	**1st Inversion**
2nd Inversion	**2nd Inversion**	**2nd Inversion**
3rd Inversion	**3rd Inversion**	**3rd Inversion**

The ninth and eleventh chords do not include the root, which is assumed to be played in the bass.

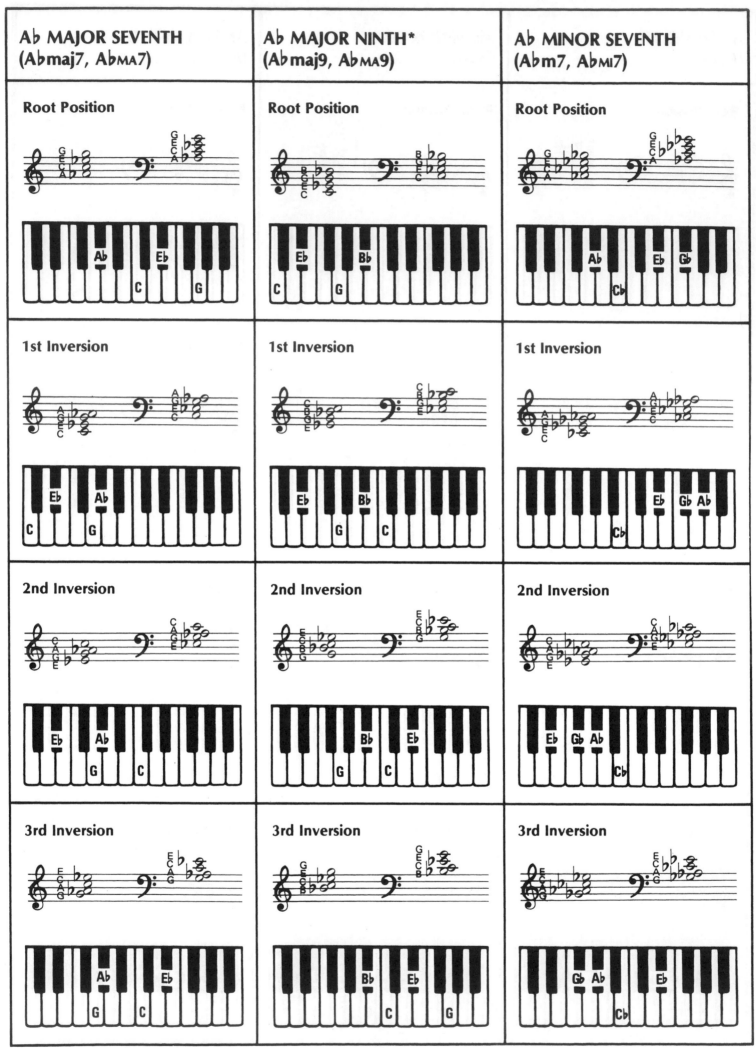

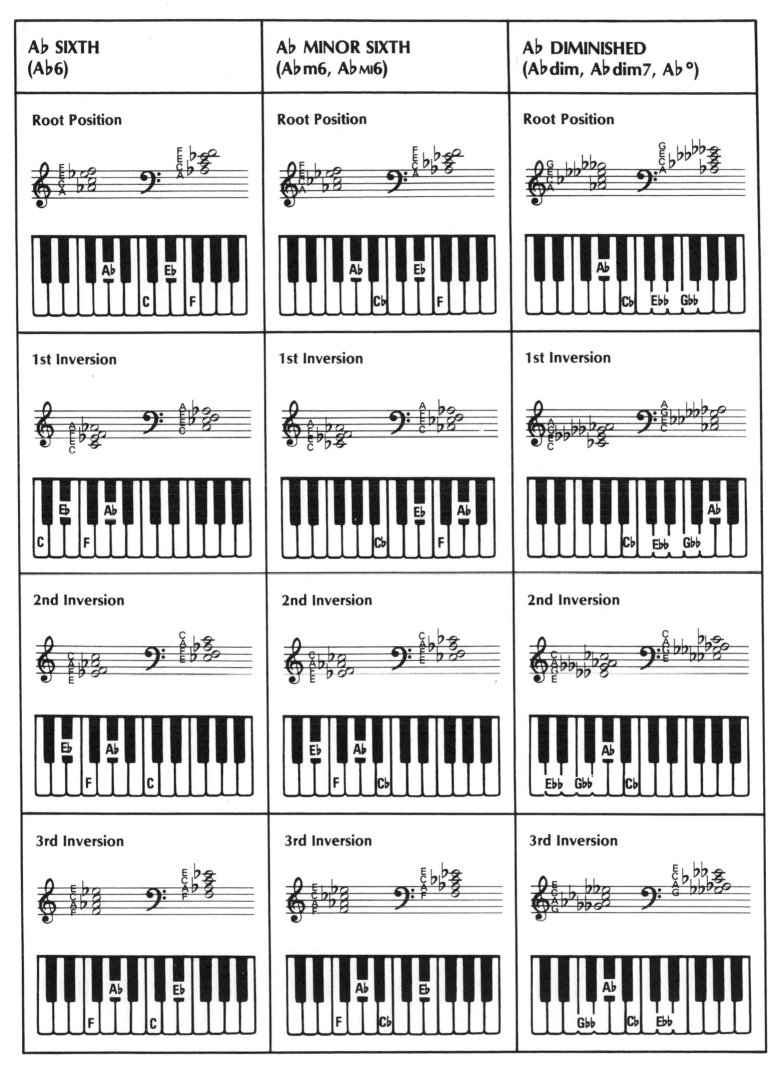

A CHORDS

A MAJOR (A)	A MINOR (Am, Ami)	A AUGMENTED (Aaug, A +)
Root Position	**Root Position**	**Root Position**
1st Inversion	**1st Inversion**	**1st Inversion**
2nd Inversion	**2nd Inversion**	**2nd Inversion**

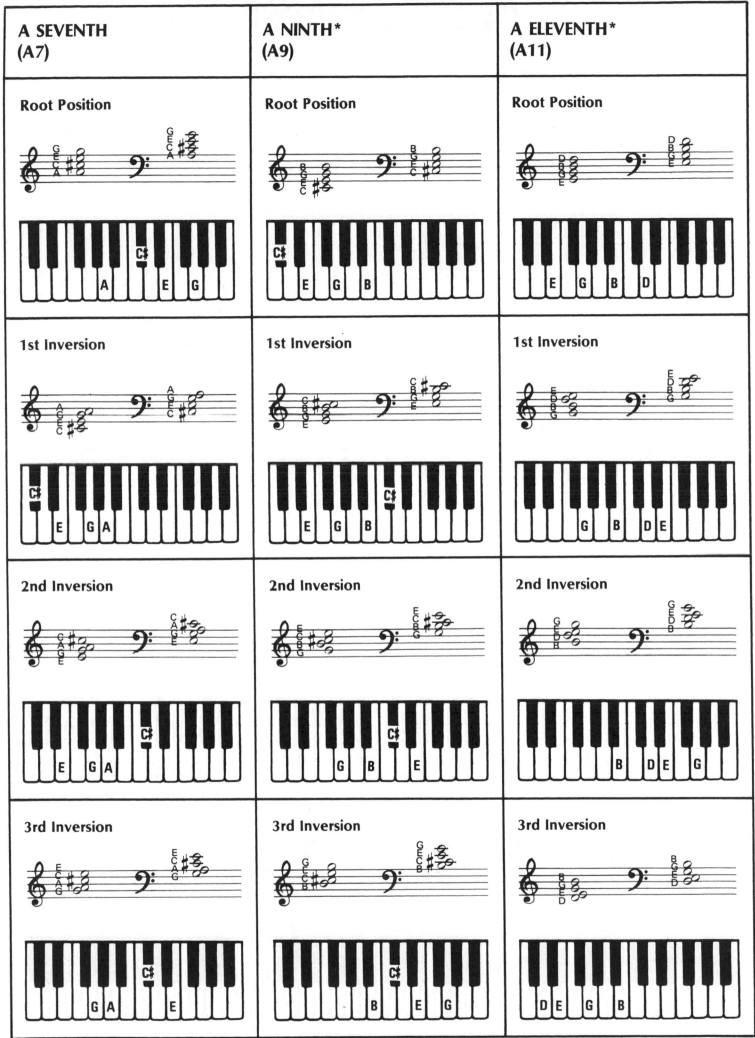

The ninth and eleventh chords do not include the root, which is assumed to be played in the bass.

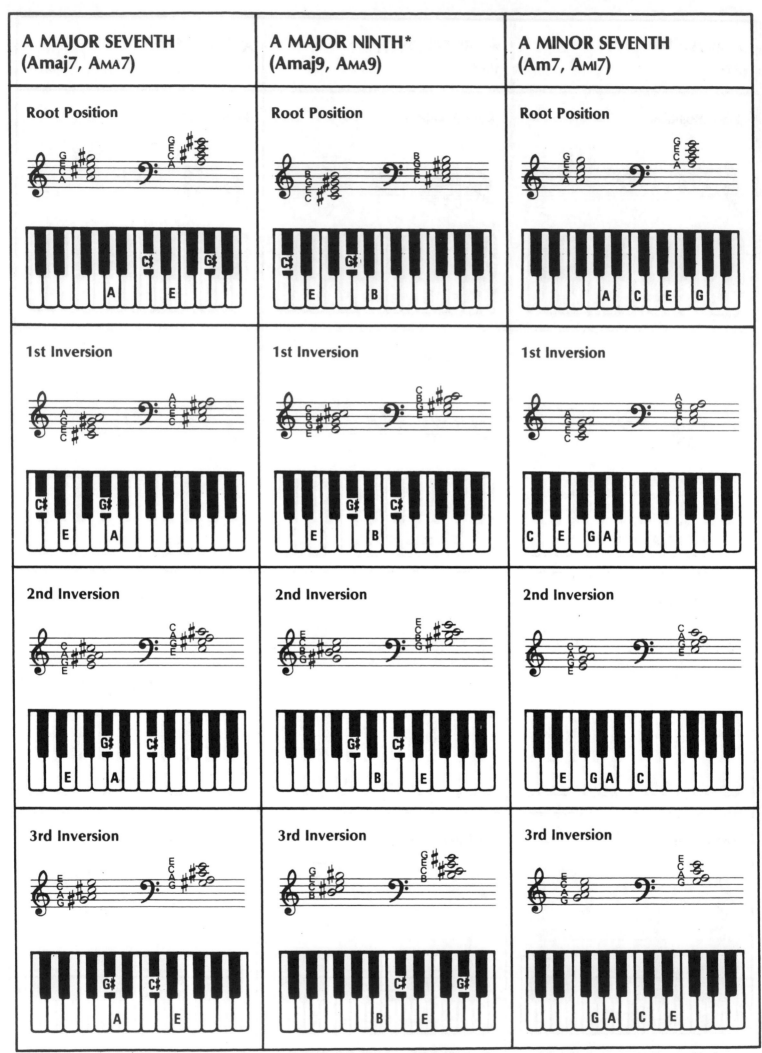

| A MAJOR SEVENTH (Amaj7, Ama7) | A MAJOR NINTH* (Amaj9, Ama9) | A MINOR SEVENTH (Am7, Ami7) |

Root Position

1st Inversion

2nd Inversion

3rd Inversion

*See note on previous page.

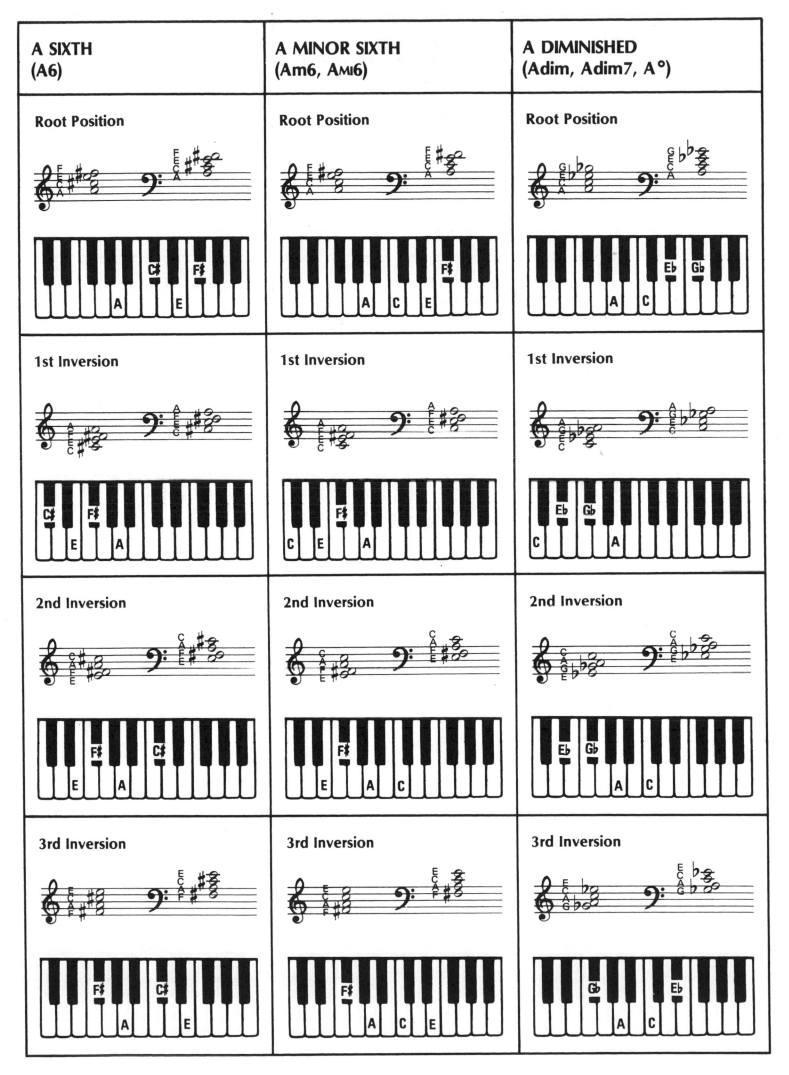

B♭ CHORDS

B♭ MAJOR (B♭)	B♭ MINOR (B♭m, B♭MI)	B♭ AUGMENTED (B♭aug, B♭ +)
Root Position	**Root Position**	**Root Position**
1st Inversion	**1st Inversion**	**1st Inversion**
2nd Inversion	**2nd Inversion**	**2nd Inversion**

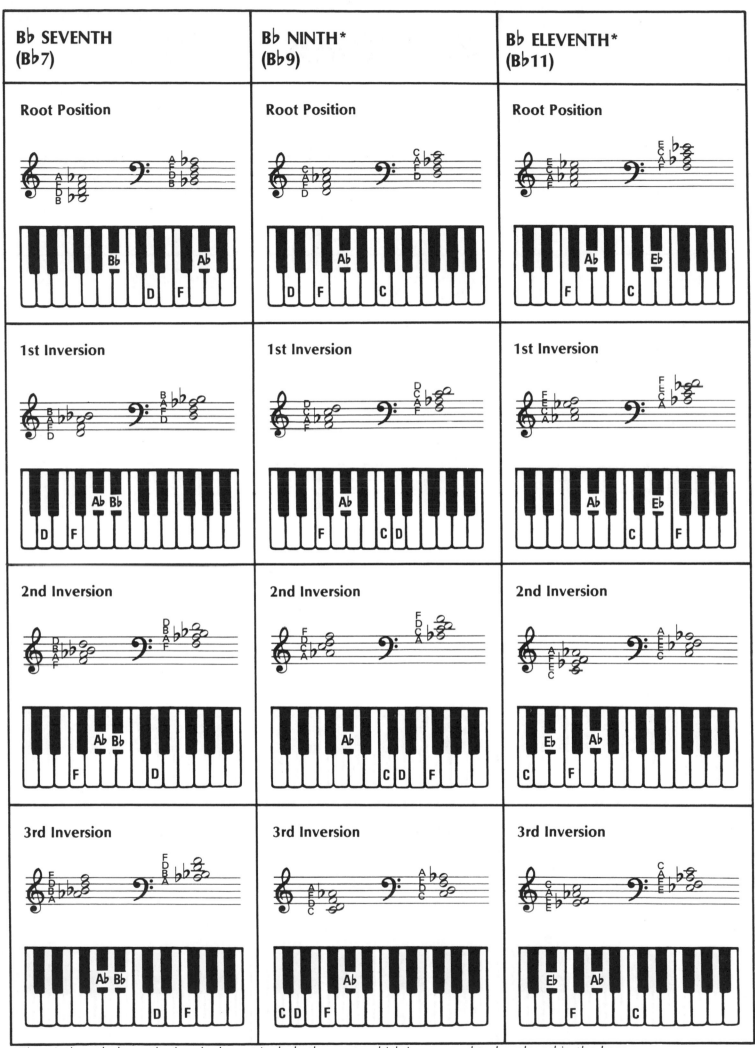

The ninth and eleventh chords do not include the root, which is assumed to be played in the bass.

Bb MAJOR SEVENTH (Bbmaj7, BbMA7)	Bb MAJOR NINTH* (Bbmaj9, BbMA9)	Bb MINOR SEVENTH (Bbm7, BbMI7)

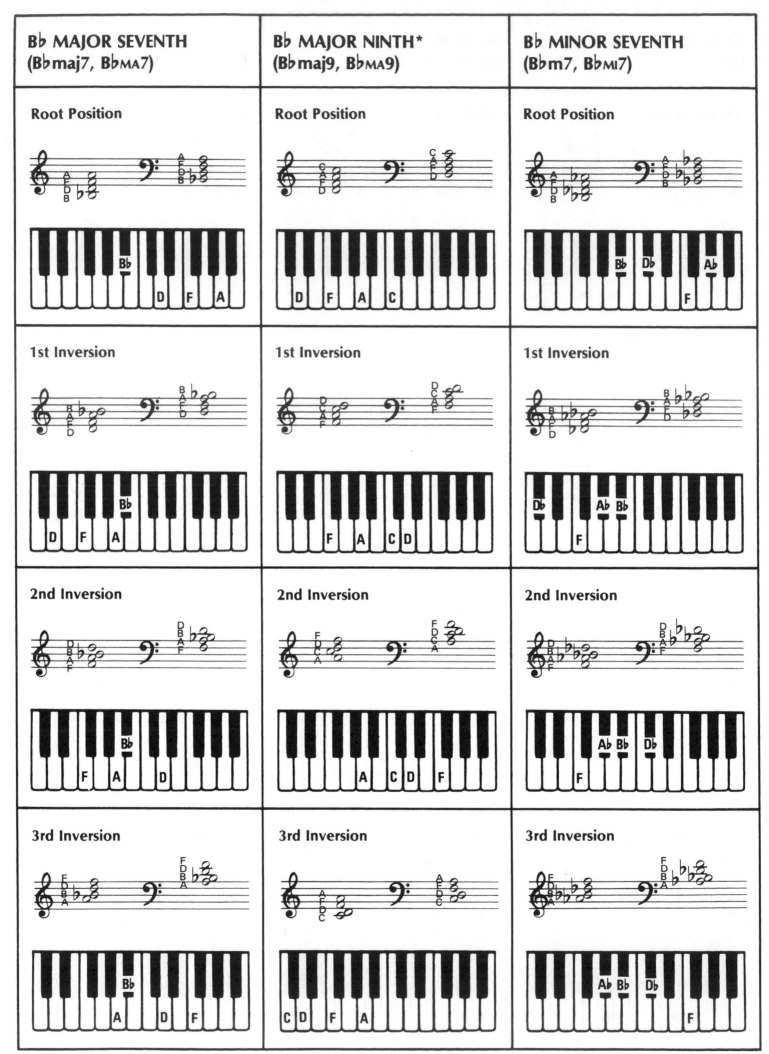

Root Position

1st Inversion

2nd Inversion

3rd Inversion

*See note on previous page.

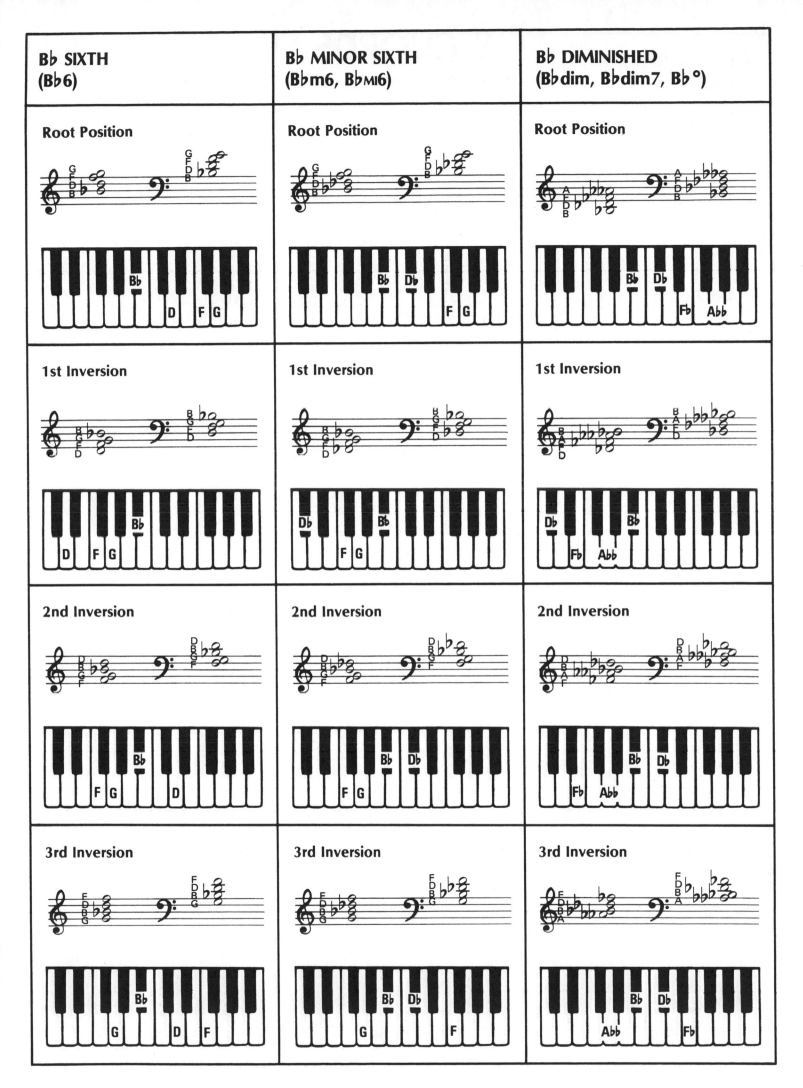

B CHORDS

B MAJOR (B)	B MINOR (Bm, BMI)	B AUGMENTED (Baug, B +)
Root Position	**Root Position**	**Root Position**
1st Inversion	**1st Inversion**	**1st Inversion**
2nd Inversion	**2nd Inversion**	**2nd Inversion**

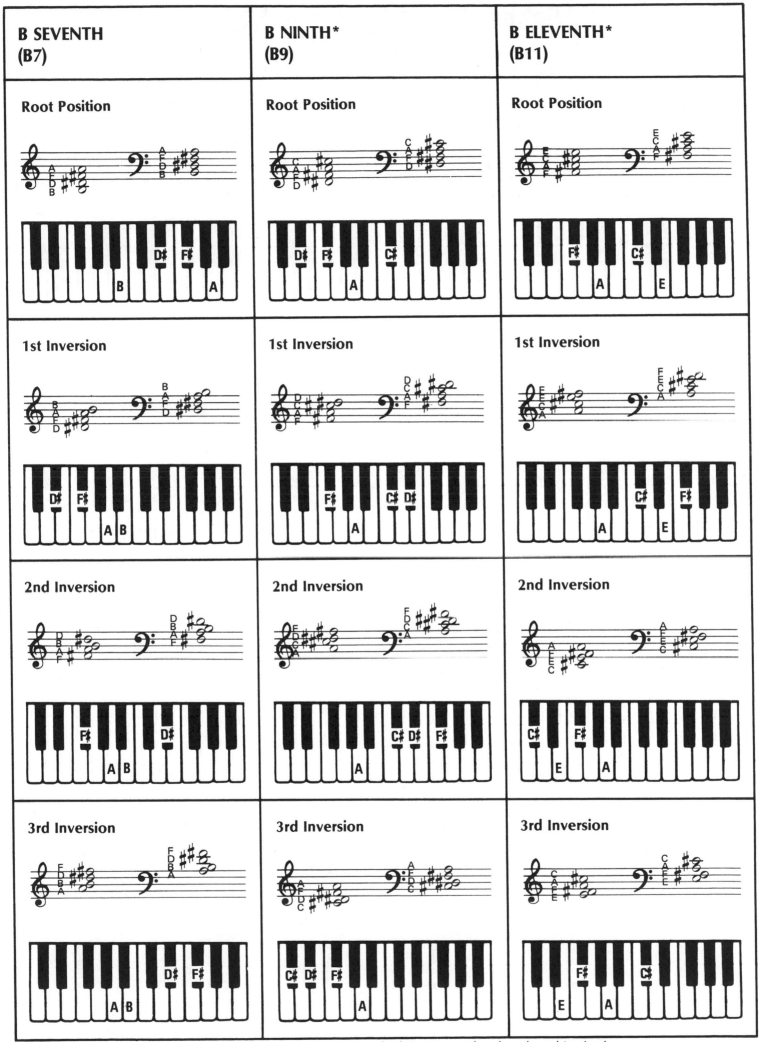

B SEVENTH (B7)	B NINTH* (B9)	B ELEVENTH* (B11)
Root Position	Root Position	Root Position
1st Inversion	1st Inversion	1st Inversion
2nd Inversion	2nd Inversion	2nd Inversion
3rd Inversion	3rd Inversion	3rd Inversion

The ninth and eleventh chords do not include the root, which is assumed to be played in the bass.

B MAJOR SEVENTH (Bmaj7, BMA7)	B MAJOR NINTH* (Bmaj9, BMA9)	B MINOR SEVENTH (Bm7, BMI7)

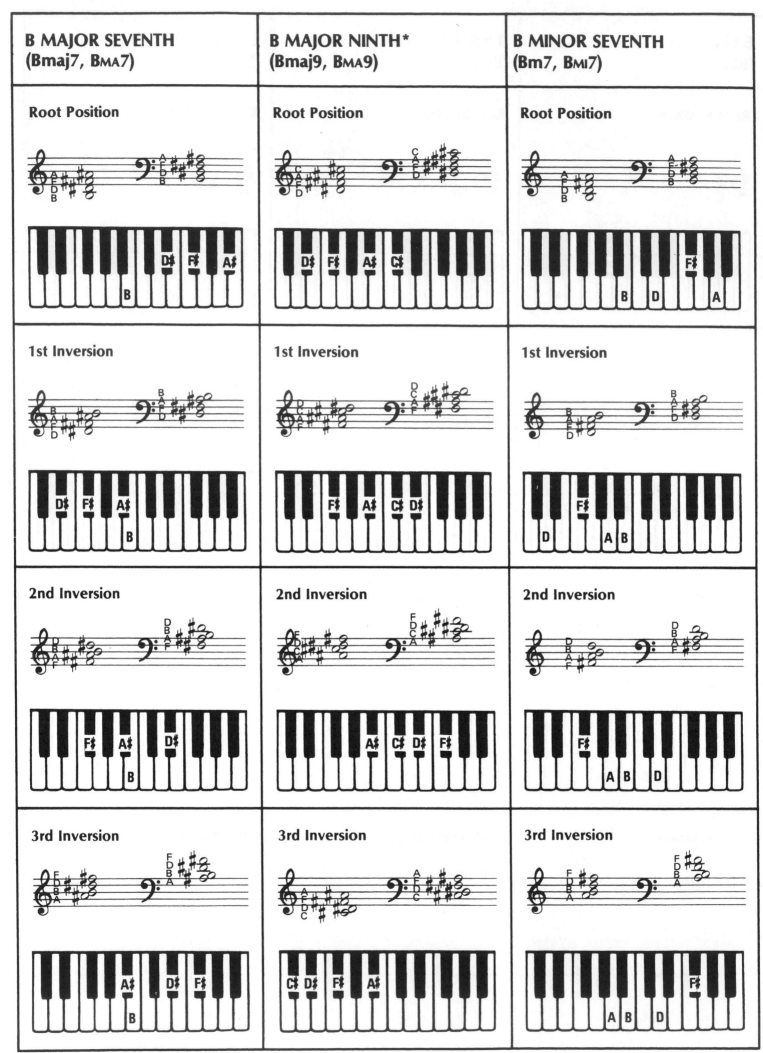

*See note on previous page.

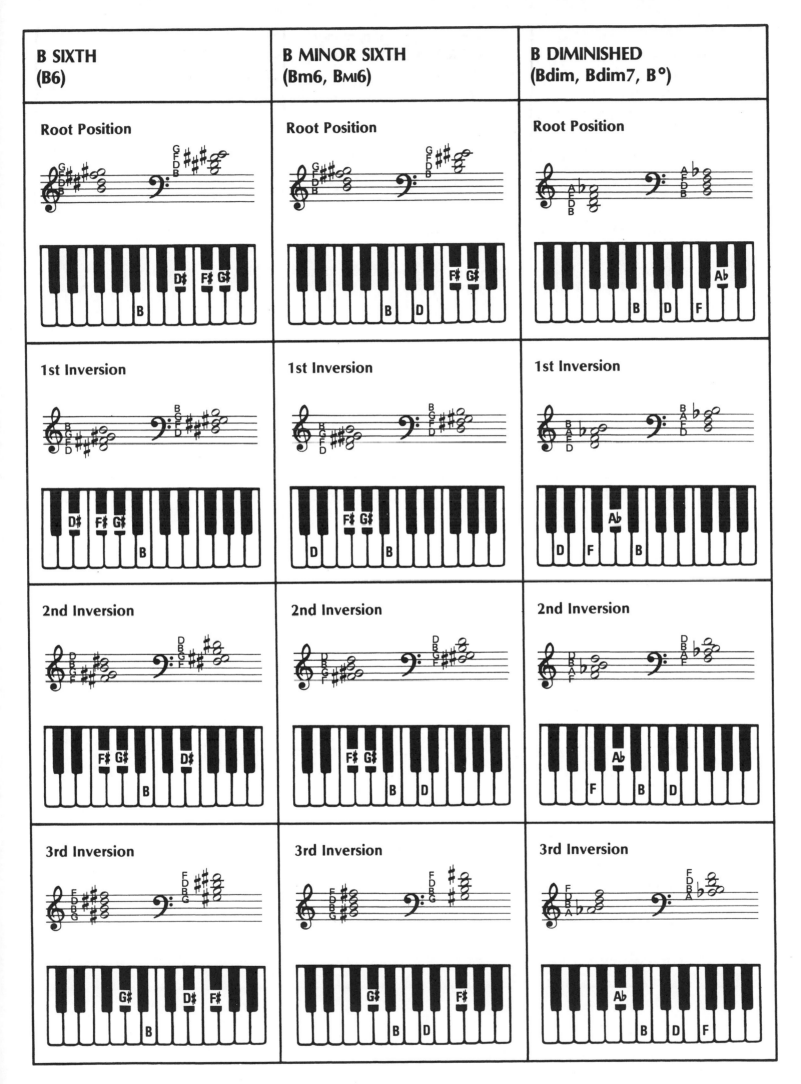

GLOSSARY

CHORD – Three or more tones played simultaneously. Chords are generally constructed using major and minor thirds.

DOUBLE FLAT (♭♭) – Indicates that a note is to be **lowered a whole step.**

DOUBLE SHARP (✕) – Indicates that a note is to be **raised a whole step.**

ENHARMONIC – Notes which are equal in pitch, but different in spelling (e.g., G♯ and A♭).

FINGERING – Finger numbers are the same for each hand, beginning with the thumb (1) and counting through the little finger (5).

FLAT (♭) – Indicates that a note is to be **lowered a half step.**

HALF STEP – The distance between two adjacent keys on the keyboard (no keys in between).

INTERVAL – The distance in pitch between two tones. The interval is named for the distance between the two note letter names. For example, the interval from A to B is a second (2 letter names), and the interval from A to G is a seventh (7 letter names).

INVERSION – Originally referred to a chord with the third, fifth, or seventh in the bass. More recently, it has come to mean a hand position where the root is not the lowest note, regardless of the true bass note.

KEY – The tonal center of a musical composition. A work is said to be in a certain key if it primarily uses the scale of the same name.

KEY SIGNATURE – The sharps or flats appearing at the beginning of a staff, which show the sharps or flats in the scale of that key.

RELATIVE MINOR – Minor key with the same key signature as a given major key. Its scale begins two scale notes below the scale of the major key. Conversely, a major key can be said to be the **relative major** of the minor key with the same key signature.

ROOT – The note on which a chord is constructed. When this note is lowest, the chord is said to be in **root position.**

SCALE – A series of notes arranged in ascending or descending order.

SHARP (♯) – Indicates that a note is to be **raised a half step.**

TONIC – The starting note of a scale. Roughly synonymous with key.

TRIAD – A three-note chord.

WHOLE STEP – The distance between two keys on the keyboard separated by a single key. Equal to two half steps.

CHORD SPELLING CHART

m = minor interval   d = diminished interval   a = augmented interval

All other intervals are major or perfect

Chord	Alternate Names	Spelling
C	CM, Cmaj., C△, Cmajor	1, 3, 5
Cm	Cmi., Cmin., C-	1, m3, 5
C+	Caug., C+5, C(♯5)	1, 3, ♯5
Cdim	C°, C diminished	1, m3, d5
Csus	Csus4	1, 4, 5
C(♭5)	C(-5)	1, 3, d5
Csus2	C2	1, 2, 5
C6	Cmaj.6, Cadd6	1, 3, 5, 6
C(add2)	C(add9)	1, 2, 3, 5
Cmaj7	C△7, CM7, CMa7	1, 3, 5, 7
Cmaj7♭5	C△7♭5, CM7(-5), Cma7(♭5)	1, 3, d5, 7
Cmaj7♯5	C△7♯5, CM7(+5), Cma7(♯5)	1, 3, a5, 7
C7	none	1, 3, 5, m7
C7♭5	C7-5	1, 3, d5, m7
C7♯5	C+7, C7+, C7+5	1, 3, a5, m7
C7sus	C7sus4	1, 4, 5, m7
Cm(add2)	Cm2, C-2	1, 2, m3, 5
Cm6	Cm(add6), C-6	1, m3, 5, 6
Cm7	C-7, Cmi7, Cmin7	1, m3, 5, m7
Cm(maj7)	C-(△7), Cmi(ma7)	1, m3, 5, 7
Cm7♭5	CØ7, Cm7-5	1, m3, d5, m7
Cdim7	C°7	1, m3, d5, d7
Cdim(maj7)	C°(maj7)	1, m3, d5, 7
C5	C(no 3rd)	1, 5
C6/9	C6/9, C6(add9)	1, 3, 5, 6, 9
Cmaj6/9	C△9(add6)	1, 3, 5, 6, 7, 9
Cmaj7♯11	C△7(♯11)	1, 3, 5, 7, all
Cmaj9	C△9, CM9, Cma9	1, 3, 5, 7, 9
Cmaj9♭5	C△9♭5, Cma9(-5)	1, 3, d5, 7, 9
Cmaj9♯5	C△9♯5, Cma9(+5)	1, 3, a5, 7, 9
Cmaj9♯11	C△9♯11, Cma9(+11)	1, 3, 5, 7, 9, a11
Cmaj13	C△13, Cma13	1, 3, 5, 7, 9, 13
Cmaj13♭5	C△13♭5, Cma13(-5)	1, 3, d5, 7, 9, 13
Cmaj13♯11	C△13♯11, Cma13(+11)	1, 3, 5, 7, 9, a11, 13
C7♭9	C7(-9)	1, 3, 5, m7, m9
C7♯9	C7(+9)	1, 3, 5, m7, a9

Chord	Alternate Names	Spelling
C7#11	C7(+11)	1, 3, 5, m7, a11
C7b5(b9)	C7(-5,-9)	1, 3, d5, m7, m9
C7b5(#9)	C7(-5,+9)	1, 3, d5, m7, a9
C7#5(b9)	C7(+5,-9)	1, 3, a5, m7, m9
C7#5(#9)	C7(+5,+9)	1, 3, a5, m7, a9
C7b9(#9)	C7(-9,+9)	1, 3, 5, m7, m9, a9
C7(add13)	C13(no 9)	1, 3, 5, m7, 13
C7b13	C7(-13)	1, 3, 5, m7, m13
C7b9(#11)	C7(-9,+11)	1, 3, 5, m7, m9, a11
C7#9(#11)	C7(+9,+11)	1, 3, 5, m7, a9, a11
C7b9(b13)	C7(-9,-13)	1, 3, 5, m7, m9, m13
C7#9(b13)	C7(+9,-13)	1, 3, 5, m7, 19, m13
C7#11(b13)	C7(+11,-13)	1, 3, 4, m7, a11, m13
C7b9(#9,#11)	C7(-9,+9,+11)	1, 3, 5, m7, m9, a9, a11
C9	none	1, 3, 5, m7, 9
C9(b5)	C9(-5)	1, 3, d5, m7, 9
C9#5	C9+, C+9	1, 3, a5, m7, 9
C9#11	C9(+11)	1, 3, 5, m7, 9, a11
C9b13	C9(-13)	1, 3, 5, m7, 9, m13
C9#11(b13)	C9(+11,-13)	1, 3, 5, m7, 9, a11, m13
C11	C9sus4, Gm7/C	1, 5, m7, 9, 11
C13	none	1, 3, 5, m7, 9, 13
C13b5	C13(-5)	1, 3, d5, m7, 9, 13
C13b9	C13(-9)	1, 3, 5, m7, m9, 13
C13#9	C13(+9)	1, 3, 5, m7, a9, 13
C13#11	C13(+11)	1, 3, 5, m7, 9, a11, 13
C13(sus4)	C13sus	1, 4, 5, m7, 9, 13
Cm(#5)	Cm+5	1, m3, a5
Cm6/9	Cmi6(add9)	1, m3, 5, 6, 9
Cm7(add4)	Cm7(add11)	1, m3, 5, m7, 11
Cm7b5(b9)	CØ7(-9)	1, m3, d5, m7, m9
Cm9	C-9, Cmin9	1, m3, 5, m7, 9
Cm9(maj7)	C-(Δ7), Cmi(ma7)	1, m3, 5, 7
Cm9(b5)	CØ9, C-7(-5)	1, m3, d5, m7, 9
Cm11	Cmin11, C-11	1, m3, 5, m7, 9, 11
Cm13	C-13, Cmin13	1, m3, 5, m7, 9, 11, 13
Cdim7(add9)	C°7(add9)	1, m3, d5, d7, 9
Cm11b5	CØ11, C-11(b5)	1, m3, d5, m7, 9, 11
Cm11(maj7)	C-11(maj7), C-11(D7)	1, m3, 5, 7, 9, 11
C7alt.	C7altered	1, 3, 5, m7, m9, a9, a11, m13

PLAY PIANO LIKE A PRO!

AMAZING PHRASING – KEYBOARD
50 Ways to Improve Your Improvisational Skills
by Debbie Denke

Amazing Phrasing is for any keyboard player interested in learning how to improvise and how to improve their creative phrasing. This method is divided into three parts: melody, harmony, and rhythm & style. The online audio contains 44 full-band demos for listening, as well as many play-along examples so you can practice improvising over various musical styles and progressions.
00842030 Book/Online Audio.............................. $16.99

BEBOP LICKS FOR PIANO
A Dictionary of Melodic Ideas for Improvisation
by Les Wise

Written for the musician who is interested in acquiring a firm foundation for playing jazz, this unique book/audio pack presents over 800 licks. By building up a vocabulary of these licks, players can connect them together in endless possibilities to form larger phrases and complete solos. The book includes piano notation, and the online audio contains helpful note-for-note demos of every lick.
00311854 Book/Online Audio.............................. $17.99

BOOGIE WOOGIE FOR BEGINNERS
by Frank Paparelli

A short easy method for learning to play boogie woogie, designed for the beginner and average pianist. Includes: exercises for developing left-hand bass • 25 popular boogie woogie bass patterns • arrangements of "Down the Road a Piece" and "Answer to the Prayer" by well-known pianists • a glossary of musical terms for dynamics, tempo and style.
00120517 .... $10.99

HAL LEONARD JAZZ PIANO METHOD
by Mark Davis

This is a comprehensive and easy-to-use guide designed for anyone interested in playing jazz piano – from the complete novice just learning the basics to the more advanced player who wishes to enhance their keyboard vocabulary. The accompanying audio includes demonstrations of all the examples in the book! Topics include essential theory, chords and voicings, improvisation ideas, structure and forms, scales and modes, rhythm basics, interpreting a lead sheet, playing solos, and much more!
00131102 Book/Online Audio.............................. $19.99

INTROS, ENDINGS & TURNAROUNDS FOR KEYBOARD
Essential Phrases for Swing, Latin, Jazz Waltz, and Blues Styles
by John Valerio

Learn the intros, endings and turnarounds that all of the pros know and use! This new keyboard instruction book by John Valerio covers swing styles, ballads, Latin tunes, jazz waltzes, blues, major and minor keys, vamps and pedal tones, and more.
00290525 .... $12.99

JAZZ PIANO TECHNIQUE
Exercises, Etudes & Ideas for Building Chops
by John Valerio

This one-of-a-kind book applies traditional technique exercises to specific jazz piano needs. Topics include: scales (major, minor, chromatic, pentatonic, etc.), arpeggios (triads, seventh chords, upper structures), finger independence exercises (static position, held notes, Hanon exercises), parallel interval scales and exercises (thirds, fourths, tritones, fifths, sixths, octaves), and more! The online audio includes 45 recorded examples.
00312059 Book/Online Audio.............................. $19.99

JAZZ PIANO VOICINGS
An Essential Resource for Aspiring Jazz Musicians
by Rob Mullins

The jazz idiom can often appear mysterious and difficult for musicians who were trained to play other types of music. Long-time performer and educator Rob Mullins helps players enter the jazz world by providing voicings that will help the player develop skills in the jazz genre and start sounding professional right away – without years of study! Includes a "Numeric Voicing Chart," chord indexes in all 12 keys, info about what range of the instrument you can play chords in, and a beginning approach to bass lines.
00310914 .... $19.99

OSCAR PETERSON – JAZZ EXERCISES, MINUETS, ETUDES & PIECES FOR PIANO

Legendary jazz pianist Oscar Peterson has long been devoted to the education of piano students. In this book he offers dozens of pieces designed to empower the student, whether novice or classically trained, with the technique needed to become an accomplished jazz pianist.
00311225 .... $14.99

PIANO AEROBICS
by Wayne Hawkins

Piano Aerobics is a set of exercises that introduces students to many popular styles of music, including jazz, salsa, swing, rock, blues, new age, gospel, stride, and bossa nova. In addition, there is a online audio with accompaniment tracks featuring professional musicians playing in those styles.
00311863 Book/Online Audio.................... $19.99

PIANO FITNESS
A Complete Workout
by Mark Harrison

This book will give you a thorough technical workout, while having fun at the same time! The accompanying online audio allows you to play along with a rhythm section as you practice your scales, arpeggios, and chords in all keys. Instead of avoiding technique exercises because they seem too tedious or difficult, you'll look forward to playing them. Various voicings and rhythmic settings, which are extremely useful in a variety of pop and jazz styles, are also introduced.
00311995 Book/Online Audio.............................. $19.99

HAL•LEONARD®
7777 W. BLUEMOUND RD. P.O. BOX 13819
MILWAUKEE, WISCONSIN 53213
www.halleonard.com

Prices, contents, and availability subject to change without notice.